Praise for *How to Grow as a Musician*

"*How to Grow as a Musician* by jazz champion, radio host, and bon vivant, Sheila Anderson is a literal life manual for the musician aspiring to a fulfilling career in jazz. With anecdotes and interviews with some of the most compelling jazz storytellers on the scene today—like Tia Fuller, Etienne Charles, Allan Harris, and Will Calhoun—and legends in the genre—like Ron Carter, Randy Weston, Al Jarreau, and Dr. Billy Taylor—Anderson shares the truth and experience in their voice and sound. This is all accomplished with warmth in her nurturing voice, while still providing nuts and bolts, 'steps 1, 2, 3,' for the musician that wants instructions on the business of jazz. [. . .] I also recommend *How to Grow as a Musician* for anyone that loves this music we call jazz to understand how to better support the musicians. In the words of my favorite jazz vocalist, Al Jarreau, as quoted in the book, 'You should always be reaching, striving for another level.' Thank you, Sheila Anderson, for taking us to ͏ ͏ er level of understanding with *How to Gro͏͏ ͏ ͏*

 —Janis Burley Wils͏͏ ͏ ͏ ͏ ͏ Wilson Center

"From the ancestors' s͏͏ ͏ ͏ ͏ ͏ ͏ ͏ ͏ ͏ ͏ing jazz musicians' experienced scen͏͏ ͏ ͏ ͏ ͏ ͏ ͏ ͏ ͏ok is an obligatory read for all musicians and creative artists looking to cultivate new sprouts for their growing careers."

       —Ron Scott, columnist, *Amsterdam News*

"For that performer who is trying to succeed in this business we call show, you need to get Sheila Anderson's book. *How to Grow as a Musician* will get you around, across, over or through any obstacle, hiccup, bump or uncertainty that may be in the way."

     —Wali Collins, author and comedian, *Coyote Ugly*,
               I Hate Valentine's Day

"This book is a must-have for any serious student and will be a joy to read by jazz fans generally. Combining a warm conversational style with the voices of musicians who provide direct, hands-on experience, it manages to be both a very practical guide and fascinating look at the music business through the eyes and words of a cross-section of accomplished musicians. Highly recommended!"

—Wayne Winborne, executive director,
Institute of Jazz Studies at Rutgers University

"This book is a must read for every aspiring musician and music fans alike. Proficient musicianship is steeped in solid practice habits, fortitude, and perseverance. Sheila exposes the fantasy that preparation can be taken lightly."

—George Wein, CEO, Festival Productions, Inc.

"Read this book to become a BAADASSSS. Sheila Anderson has told it like it is."

—Melvin Van Peebles, filmmaker

"Sheila Anderson is a living legend in the world of jazz radio whose vision, wisdom, and knowledge are astonishing. Don't miss this book!"

—Cornel West, professor emeritus, Princeton University

"*How to Grow as a Musician* is both intelligent and comprehensive. Ms. Anderson offers an insightful and timely roadmap for one's career."

—Gregory Generet, jazz vocalist

HOW TO GROW AS A MUSICIAN

SECOND EDITION

HOW TO GROW AS A MUSICIAN

SECOND EDITION

What All Musicians Must Know to Succeed

SHEILA E. ANDERSON

ALLWORTH PRESS
NEW YORK

Allworth Press books may be purchased in bulk at special discounts for sales
promotion, corporate gifts, fund-raising, or educational purposes. Special
editions can also be created to specifications. For details, contact the Special Sales
Department, Allworth Press, 307 West 36th Street, 11th Floor, New York, NY
10018 or info@skyhorsepublishing.com.

23 22 21   5 4 3 2

Published by Allworth Press, an imprint of Skyhorse Publishing, Inc. 307 West
36th Street, 11th Floor, New York, NY 10018. Allworth Press® is a registered
trademark of Skyhorse Publishing, Inc.®, a Delaware corporation.

www.allworth.com

Cover design by Mary Ann Smith

Library of Congress Cataloging-in-Publication Data is available on file.

Print ISBN: 978-1-62153-716-8
eBook ISBN: 978-1-62153-718-2

Printed in the United States of America

DEDICATION

In loving memory of my mom, Daisy Estelle Anderson (February 14, 1922–July 29, 2019), who taught me to have confidence and gave me the tools for success. She was driven, determined, and an inspiration to so many—a true role model!

And to Johnnie Garry (October 31, 1924—March 13, 2018), a mentor to me and a force in the jazz community, who Duke Ellington nicknamed Ziegfeld. To quote Duke, "We love you madly."

Contents

Contents

ACKNOWLEDGMENTS

With gratitude I thank Tad Crawford for allowing me to write this revision. To my editor, Chamois Holschuh, thank you for your patience and guidance. Thanks to my WBGO family for their support. And to Brian Delp, who kept me company through the night serenading me with the great music.

Introduction

In 2004, when I was working on the first edition of this book, I wanted to interview Will Calhoun. After a few failed attempts to set a time to talk, we agreed to speak, one morning, at 1:00 a.m. (I recall that he was preparing for a trip.) On schedule, I called, he didn't answer, so I left a message and moved on. Shortly after the book's publication, I ran into Will sitting at the bar in the jazz club the Village Vanguard. How we began our conversation is vague, but I do recall him asking me, "What about my comments in your book?" Needless to say, given that the interview had not transpired, I was stunned he would ask me about it; I reminded him that he and I had not spoken, so he wasn't *in* my book. Will laughed, then said, "I'll be in your next book." My retort to him: "What makes you think that there *will* be a next one?" He said, "There will be." I marveled at his confidence. Over these years, he and I have become great friends. A man of many talents, not only is Will Calhoun a great musician, he is also a visual artist. He is an intellect, a spiritual man, a loving father and husband, whose passion for music and reverence of the ancestors is inspiring. Is he clairvoyant? Perhaps. When I told him that my publisher agreed to allow me to write this second edition, he wasn't surprised; remember, he had predicted that in 2005.

In addition to Will Calhoun, I have added new voices: musicians Etienne Charles, Jeremy Pelt, Tia Fuller, Camille Thurman, Javon Jackson, Aaron Diehl, Ulysses Owens Jr., Mikael Karlsson, and Monte Croft. For a follow-up, I talked with Allan Harris, Eric Reed, Dorothy Lawson, Michael Wolff, Bobby Sanabria, and WBGO music director and radio personality Gary Walker. The other two radio professionals interviewed are Derrick Lucas (Jazz 90.1) and Terrence McKnight of WQXR. Last, publicist Gwendolyn Quinn gave me a crash course on her profession. From the first edition I kept some information from the interviews of Kenny Barron, Andy Bey, Ron Carter, Jeff Clayton, Paula Kimper, Richard Smallwood, and Kenny Washington (the drummer). After the first printing, fourteen years have passed. Several people I had interviewed have died: Oscar Brown Jr., Ruth Brown, Edwin Hawkins, Al Jarreau, John Levy, David Randolph, and Dr. Billy Taylor. To preserve their memories, I dedicate the last chapter, "Ancestors: So Past, So Present—Standing on Their Shoulders," to them.

Since 2005, the business has drastically changed. The vibrant club scene has diminished. At that time, the digital age was nascent but is now our reality and can't be ignored. Popular since 1985, in February and March of 2008, "smooth jazz" stations in New York and Washington, DC, shifted formats to rock, leaving two of the nation's largest radio markets free of Kenny G, Chris Botti, Dave Koz, and Spyro Gyra. A sea change occurred on July 1, 2002, with the launch of the groundbreaking satellite SIRIUS radio. Its business model was pay-for-service radio. Music channels were presented without advertising, and all channels were free of FCC regulations. Just like cable TV, a separate unit was required to use the service. The positive and negative impact of the digital age on content and musicians can't be overstated, and that's why I have devoted some chapters addressing issues related to musician royalties, recordings, and consumer consumption. As in the first edition, the book has six sections: "On Development as an Artist," "On Composing, Arranging, and Recording," "On Personal Growth," "On Performance Etiquette," "On the Business," and "The Empty-Vessel Theory." Because much of our communication and interaction takes place through our mobile devices, the business section now includes information on social media and streaming, as well as a chapter titled "The Art of 'The Hang.'" At the end of each chapter, I added notes, which summarize key points for your reference. This book is intended for musicians and nonmusicians alike. Regardless of industry, everyone should learn their craft, educate themselves, look for work, and gauge personal and professional progress.

This is my story. Though I may "play" one on the radio, I am not a musician. I own a flute and a piano! Music has always been in my blood. Perhaps if I'd had the discipline, I may have become one given my proclivity for music. I was born and raised in Buffalo, New York, into one of the city's oldest black families (my father's great-grandfather, Ben Taylor, moved there in 1832). In the early 1940s, my mother moved from Terre Haute, Indiana, and met my dad; six months later, they were married. Both parents come from educated people. Not only was my dad's Aunt Emilia the secretary of the Niagara Movement—the precursor to the NAACP—she was also the first African American student to graduate from Syracuse University. My mother's mom graduated at the top in her class at Fisk University, and her dad was a graduate of Purdue University. Education was paramount in my household. When I was in first or second grade, my dad began his undergraduate studies, and he received his law degree when I was a sophomore in high school. My mom got her master's degree when I was young.

There was never a question that I would go to college, but unlike my three siblings, I struggled through school. To my parents' dismay, my focus was more on socializing, less on the academics. (Basically, I was what one would describe as "a party animal." I was great at organizing parties, and I was the resident DJ. I had a unit that was a combination turntable and cassette player. I'd use my headphones to cue up the songs for a smooth transition.) My interests centered on politics, music, art, literature, and being around creative people. This may come as a surprise to some, but I was an introvert at heart. Uncertain of my life path, I read several self-help books for inspiration, such as *The Magic of Believing*, *The Power of Positive Thinking*, and *In Search of the Meaning of Life*. Music was always in our home.

If a record wasn't spinning on our stereo, someone was playing an instrument. We had a piano that Mom played; on occasion, Uncle Jerry would come and play it. My oldest brother, "Chips," had a great record collection that included music from Miles Davis to Lead Belly. Around age seven, the first time I heard Miles Davis's *E.S.P.* and Richard "Groove" Holmes's *Soul Message*, I was hooked. Mom's taste in music was equally eclectic. Because we had only *one* record player, Sunday was *her* day to listen to *her* music, which ranged from Duke Ellington and Mahalia Jackson to classical music and Joan Baez.

We all had to take up an instrument, and Mom sent us to the Community School of Music, where I took theory. Before settling on the flute, I played the recorder. (My piano skills were negligible, but I did OK on the guitar. In the junior high school band, I actually played the glockenspiel.) I fell in love with the flute and dreamed of becoming the next Bobbi Humphrey. My plans to become a musician were thwarted when I got involved with the NAACP as a teen. Turning my attention to work in the civil rights organization, first as local youth president, then, at sixteen, as New York State Youth President, ending with my election to the National Board at age nineteen, I chose to not devote the needed time and work that would set me on the path to be a musician.

For various reasons, I did not go directly to college after my high school graduation. Instead, I stayed in Buffalo, got a job, and attended classes at three different institutions of higher learning. Frustrated by living in Buffalo, at twenty-one, I decided to move to New York City with the intention of getting my degree and returning home. John Lennon said, "Life is what happens to you while you're busy making other plans." That pretty much sums up *my* life! Life in New York City wasn't easy. Though it took me longer than anticipated, I did graduate from Baruch College when I was thirty-two.

I got my first full-time job working in publishing at Random House as a production assistant. Ultimately, I loved my colleagues and being in the industry, but I didn't enjoy the work. When asked, I accepted the secretary position in the Bookbinder's Guild (now the Book Industry Guild of New York) and worked my way into the presidency eight years later. Finding myself at a crossroads, I looked to find a different line of work. I considered getting a degree in social work. I went to bartending school. I attended modeling school (on the suggestion of my mother), but nothing came out of any of these things. In 1987, I started to volunteer for WBGO. It was great to connect with people who shared my love of jazz and to be around a public radio station in its infancy. Seeing my interest in the music and a slight desire to be on air (I had done some radio work in college), one of the announcers insisted that I talk to Thurston Briscoe, then the programming director, about getting an on-air job. I mustered up the courage to talk with him. To my surprise, he gave me permission to go in and learn how to operate the board. It took about three years before a slot opened up for *Sunday Morning Harmony* (6:00 a.m. to 10:00 a.m.). In November 1994, Thurston asked me to do the show temporarily, while he was looking for a permanent host. My first on-air shift was the overnight, February 15, 1995.

Having had *no* on-air experience, the first several years, I must admit, were painful. I had a good feel for the music, but my announcing skills were abysmal. I'm grateful to Thurston and all of the other announcers for helping me work on my delivery. In addition to my poor delivery, I had gaps in my jazz knowledge and thought it best that I learn about the music from the musicians. Other than *Singers Unlimited*, interviews weren't allowed during weekend shows. In 1993, I trained at the local cable TV station, Manhattan Neighborhood Network (MNN), to do a show. Unable to produce the show I had in mind, I decided to do a jazz-interview show that I called *The Art of Jazz*. However, I didn't know many musicians, so my challenge was to meet some. I took myself to the famed club Bradley's, sat at the bar, and introduced myself to every musician who was there and invited them to be my guest. From that point, I immersed myself in the community, and I haven't looked back. I knew that I wanted to work around creative people, that I loved music, and that I am a social being. Through trial and error, highs and lows, I have been able to create a life and a living in a world that I dreamed of.

PART ONE

ON DEVELOPMENT AS AN ARTIST

The mastership in music, and in life, in fact,
is not something that can be taught—it can only be caught.
—Rodney Jones

CHAPTER 1

Getting Started

Does this sound familiar? You have decided to become a musician; music is your life, and all you want to do is play, play, play. At some point you asked yourself, or someone else, which steps are needed to turn your dream into a reality. The first thing you should determine is if you want to use music as a vehicle for financial gain or if you want a career. Those interviewed for this book have chosen to build a career. Benjamin Franklin purportedly said, "If you fail to plan, you are planning to fail." To make a plan is good advice, but how you "work" your plan is equally important. The outspoken filmmaker Melvin Van Peebles told me, "Early to bed, early to rise, work like a dog, and advertise." The bottom line is that you should have a plan. Know what you want to do and where you want to do it. Learn to be flexible, and give yourself permission to change as you grow.

No matter your career choice, you should learn your craft. As it relates to musicians, famed jazz drummer Kenny Washington put an emphasis on experience. He learned by listening to records, by taking classes, by being mentored, by "learning as he went," and/or by working with different types of musicians. He advises that "it is important to tell musicians: Study the music, get a good teacher, listen to the musicians and players that came before you. Never let anyone tell

3

you it's old fashioned. Don't be afraid to copy any of the musicians. You must sound like others before you sound like yourself. In classical music, you have to go back; in jazz, the young people don't know nearly as much as they should about this music, and it's a disgrace. Learn standards; when the record company drops you, you'll have to be a sideman."

I implore you to work as often as you can. Take low-paying gigs, work for tips, and go to jam sessions, because the more you work, the better you will get. You will acquire more knowledge about the music as well as about the business. For ten years, I worked as the emcee for the summer Jazzmobile concerts on Wednesday evenings at Grant's Tomb, without pay. That experience was invaluable! The musicians interviewed shared their journeys of hard work and dedication. Again, "early to bed . . ." What they have in common are passion, drive, determination, and fortitude as they navigate the business. The path isn't easy, nor is it straight. Life is filled with ups and downs, highs and lows, and there are no guarantees. So, why not follow your passion? Todd Barkan, a jazz impresario and producer, at the end of each concert that he emceed, would say, "Take care of the music, it will take care of you."

HOW THEY GOT STARTED

Will Calhoun

Will Calhoun, the widely acclaimed drummer from the Bronx, New York, graduated from the Berklee School of Music in Boston, where he received a bachelor's degree in music production and engineering. He became a household name as the drummer for the rock band Living Colour. His unique blend of improvisational and hard rock drumming can be found on each of Living Colour's four Epic releases: the groundbreaking multiplatinum debut *Vivid*, the critically acclaimed sophomore LP *Time's Up*, the *Biscuits* EP, and *Stain*, as well as their latest release on Sanctuary Records, *CollideØscope*. A prolific songwriter, Will has cowritten many Living Colour compositions and wrote the critically acclaimed song "Pride" on the *Time's Up* album and "Nothingness" on the *Stain* album. As a member of

Living Colour, Will received two Grammy Awards for Best Hard Rock Performance by a group. They also won an International Rock Award for Best Rock Band.

The time was ripe for the rock and roll group to exist in the mid-1980s. They had an arena where they could put forth their talents. Other rock bands were working then, and classic rock radio existed (1975–1990). Will met Vernon Reid (leader of Living Colour) when he was doing a radio show with Greg Tate. They had previously met, briefly, one time, during one of Will's Berklee College breaks. Will had played with Jaco Pastorius, who asked if he knew Vernon and told him he had to hook them up. After leaving Berklee, Will went back to New York City and ran into Vernon, where they exchanged tapes of their groups—Will's Dark Sarcasm and Vernon's Colours. They discovered a shared interest. Will recalled,

> At that time English rockers were coming and taking the best black rock musicians, so Vernon lost lots of band members. Vernon decided to put together a group who had a focus, and that's when we formed Living Colour. . . . It didn't take a long time, in the scheme of things, for the group to take off, about four years. We treated the band like a job (we weren't making any money) with daily rehearsals, etc. I was living at home and asked his mom if she'd give him a year; if I failed I'd get a job. Word traveled that we were hot, and we started playing at CBGB's. Mick Jagger came to see us when he was in town. . . . I was never afraid that it wouldn't happen for us."

The rest, as they say, is history.

www.willcalhoun.com

Ron Carter

Carter is among the most original, prolific, and influential bassists in jazz history, with more than 2,200 albums to his credit, an accomplishment honored in the 2015 *Guinness Book of World Records*. He has recorded with greats including Tommy Flanagan, Gil Evans, Lena Horne, Bill Evans, B. B. King, the Kronos Quartet, Dexter Gordon, Wes Montgomery, Bobby Timmons, Jaki Byard, Eric Dolphy, and Cannonball Adderley. In 2014, Ron received the medallion and title of "Commander of the Order of Arts and Letters," France's premier cultural award, given by the French minister of culture. Ron Carter has been a world-class bassist and cellist since the 1960s. He's among the greatest accompanists of all time, but he has also done many albums exhibiting his prodigious technique. Carter is nearly as accomplished in classical music as he is in jazz, and he has performed with symphony orchestras all over the world. He played in the Eastman School's Philharmonic Orchestra and gained his degree in 1959. He joined Art Farmer's group for a short time in 1963, before he was tapped to become a member of Miles Davis's band. Carter remained with Davis until 1968. He is possibly the most recorded bassist in jazz history. He has led his own bands at various intervals since 1972. As a leader, he has recorded over fifty albums. Carter also contributed many arrangements and compositions to both his own groups and to other bands. He even invented his own instrument, a piccolo bass. His recordings have encompassed an unusually imaginative range of ideas—from cello ensembles to reexaminations of Bach.

A best-selling author, Carter's books include *Building Jazz Bass Lines* and his autobiography *Finding the Right Notes*. In 2016, he published *Ron Carter's Comprehensive Bass Method*, an advanced-level book pioneering the use of QR codes to demonstrate technique in printed books. Additionally, Ron authored *The Ron Carter Songbook*, a collection of 119 original compositions. In 2017, Ron expanded his reach to his considerable worldwide following on Facebook, where he regularly posts helpful information and backstories for bass players and fans alike. His "Facebook Live" events are enjoyed around the world. Ron teaches frequently at master classes internationally. He has also received five honorary doctorates, most recently from The Juilliard School.

He was hooked from the beginning. "When I was ten years old, I had my first lesson on cello, and I thought this was for me." Though he does not like to talk about his transition to jazz, he did reluctantly and briefly:

> I wanted to be a classical cello player. To be a jazz musician didn't come along until much later. . . . Well, when I was in Detroit, my saxophone player neighbor liked Paul Desmond, Dave Brubeck. At the time, they had a big hit, *Jazz at the College*, in 1954 on Fantasy. There were a lot of sorority/fraternity dances on these big boats, and he knew somebody who did these bookings, and he told the guy to get a band in to play for the dances. So he got together myself, and a piano player and drummer, and had rehearsals and made these boat rides out in Belle Isle. I was a classical cello player. I went to string bass because I thought all the white guys were getting all the gigs. As a classical bass player, I saw all the auditions were being steered toward the white bass players in school. And then in my senior year in college, I was in the orchestra, and the guest conductor told me he would love to have me in his orchestra, but that the board directors weren't hiring colored musicians. That was 1958–1959. I went back to New York. The Philharmonic had no black people, maybe one. So I thought, let me do something else, then. I decided to go to Manhattan School of Music. I had a full scholarship to go to Manhattan in 1960 upon graduation from college. When I got to New York, I met Chico Hamilton in Rochester during a concert, and he told me when I got to New York, if he was working around town, come to say hello. Well, actually, I auditioned for him as a cello player, but the cello player decided to stay in the band. When I got to New York, the bass player quit. So I joined the band as a bass player with Eric Dolphy. I played with Randy Weston for almost a year, a couple of years, and Bobby Timmons, Betty Carter, Herbie Mann, and so on and so forth.

Etienne Charles

Trumpeter/bandleader/composer/educator Charles is one of the most compelling and exciting young jazz artists ushering the genre into groundbreaking new territory as a trumpeter/bandleader. He was born on July 24, 1983. While in his twenties, he recorded seven impressive and well-received albums for his own "Culture Shock Music" imprint. His new album, *Creole Soul*, is a captivating journey of new jazz expression. It buoyantly taps into a myriad of styles rooted in his Afro-Caribbean background and plumbs the musical depths of the islands, from calypso to Haitian voodoo music. Also in the jazz amalgam mix are rocksteady, reggae, Kongo, and rock as well as the influence of Motown and R&B music Charles listened to on his parents' record player when he was growing up.

> I'm a musician, only thing I wanted to do (from twelve years of age). I was around lots of musicians growing up, but lots of them had day jobs, but I knew that it was what I wanted to do but I now teach, as well. I've been teaching ten years at Michigan State University (MSU). They reached out to me, indirectly, then I submitted an application and I won out after three finalists. I love it. I freelanced in New York for one year after I graduated from school (BA Florida State), did my MA at Juilliard . . . came to New York City to work and to get my master's degree.

While attending college, Etienne gigged at night, though he had had a head start leading bands while in undergrad at Florida State.

> In Florida a friend got me working while I was in my freshman year. He was a bass player and got a gig at a restaurant where we played for tips. Tallahassee restaurants had all their windows and doors open, so lots of people came in and out and we made lots of money from tips. My buddy moved to California so they asked me to take over the gig and then I became a leader. Then I got lots of gigs,

weddings, etc. Got into contracting. I learned how to get a band paid, how to set up the band and I was learning to be a manager. I did that for three or four years . . . [famed pianist] Marcus Roberts would sub out a gig, too. When I moved to New York the first day I had a record date with Ralph MacDonald, Buddy Williams was on drums. That was August 26, 2006. I had met Buddy and Ralph before—they told me to call them when I got to New York City. Buddy told me to join the union. Kamau Adilifu called me for the gig—*The Color Purple*—and I got on the sub list. Then I got called to do one night then folks have to sign off on you to get the gig. I subbed for Kamau then got to sub for others and was in school and doing the show. Made sure I lived near the subway so I could get to gigs quick and have my phone on. Have to get to a place in thirty to sixty minutes top. Subbed at Swing 46, a gospel funk band, and we were busy on the weekends. Then more weddings and corporate gigs so I worked steadily so money came from different sources. Then I got a job programming at JALC in summertime and I put a group together to play that—Brian Hogans, Marion Felder, Robert Rodriguez, and Ralph MacDonald—things just took off . . .

www.etiennecharles.com

Jeff Clayton

Jeff Clayton straddled genres and continues to do so, although he is primarily considered a jazz musician.

I began in jazz music; it is the art of being a chameleon, it is so special, it prepares you to do any music. You steal solos, jazz, funk, or classical music; you just copy and mimic that. Then you understand the parameters of these styles, and good jazz musicians can copy. I started out on Concord Records as a jazz artist, then I did pop because someone asked me if I could, so I stole some solos, learned some songs of Stevie Wonder from his records until I knew how to play pop. When I did that, I changed the way I played in my mind and body and played pop. When I stopped playing pop, I turned on jazz and classical; they are closely related.

Clayton was born in Venice, California, and his musical education began at a local Baptist church, where his mother was the pianist and conductor of the choir. He began playing various reed instruments, including the clarinet, but he concentrated on alto saxophone. He later added the soprano saxophone and the flute, extending his studies during his high school and university education, in which his principal instrument was the oboe. He dropped out of the university before graduating in order to go on the road with Stevie Wonder. Later, he mixed studio work with touring, playing with artists as diverse as Gladys Knight, Kenny Rogers, Patti LaBelle, and Michael Jackson. He gradually shifted toward a more jazz-oriented repertoire, and although he continued to work in orchestras backing popular singers such as Frank Sinatra, Mel Tormé, Lena Horne, and Sammy Davis Jr., it was in the jazz world that he established his reputation during the eighties. He played in the Tommy Dorsey Orchestra under the direction of Murray McEachern, with Count Basie; the continuing Basie band under Thad Jones; and with Alphonse Mouzon, Juggernaut, Woody Herman, Lionel Hampton, Ella Fitzgerald, the Phillip Morris Superband led by Gene Harris, Monty Alexander, Ray Brown, and many others. Clayton continued to work with pop stars, playing saxophone solos on the *Dick Tracy* (1990) soundtrack album and on Madonna's companion album to the film (*I'm Breathless*). Clayton has worked extensively in partnership with his brother, John Clayton, and the Claytons are also active in the big band they colead, the Clayton-Hamilton Jazz Orchestra, with drummer Jeff Hamilton, as well as the Clayton Brothers Quintet. In 2019, Jeff recorded *Through the Looking Glass*, his first CD under his own name.

Monte Croft

A thirty-five-year-plus veteran of the New York music scene, Croft is a multi-instrumentalist, playing six instruments and counting: drums, vibraphone, keyboards, chromatic harmonica, bass guitar, and guitar. Part of Monte's arsenal includes his voice, which brings the count to seven instruments. A brief stint at Columbia Records in the eighties produced two highly acclaimed albums—*A Higher Fire* and *Survival of the Spirit*. Monte has performed and recorded with diverse artists, including Gladys Knight, Nicholas Payton, Gino Vannelli, Hubert Laws, and P. Diddy. In 2012, he was a member of the classic, platinum-selling R&B/funk unit the Average White Band. He also worked in television and on Broadway. Monte has become a staple at Ashford and Simpson's Sugar Bar in New York City.

> I consider myself both: a leader and a sideman. I play R&B, jazz, I don't have a problem with the label jazz musician. I wasn't encouraged to make music a career. Berklee, Juilliard, Eastman, North Texas State were focused on jazz when I came along, and Dana School of Music in my hometown, Youngstown, Ohio, had a great program, too. My band director had been right out of college. (I didn't know what I wanted to do but I wanted to stay in music. I knew I had more to learn and wanted to go to college.) My teacher suggested that I check out Berklee.

After two and a half years, Monte chose to leave Berklee and return to Ohio: "I had a good experience there and got so much information. . . . It's taken years to process some of it. The energy and vibe is just want I needed to see." He was happy to be around people who were encouraged to be musicians and were his age. It was push and pull for him growing up; whether to do or not to do. To be a musician was "my heart's dream, I didn't want to let it go and why I grabbed Berklee and the East Coast seemed appealing." His reason for leaving college was "I left, got out of Dodge. I left because I wanted to practice and went back to Ohio for one year but was there two and a half years, stayed with my folks . . ." That respite left him restless, so he chose to go to New York City: "I had friends there and family so it took the fear out of being there." Monte has no regrets that he didn't finish: "Depends on the day, but I'm doing what I want to do, but I like to play." Unlike a lot of his contemporaries, he had a lot of day jobs and is amazed that he knows guys who never had day jobs. "I'd ask, 'how did you manage to not do that,'" he chuckles.

> My first steady job in New York City was working at ASCAP. Though music related, it really wasn't. Actually, a music-related job is not necessarily the best job for a musician, because it just heightens the frustration cause you're seemingly close to it (playing) but you're really not. I sat at a desk all day and listened to tapes. I'd fall asleep every day too, because I was hanging out every night at jam sessions at night. I also did clerk jobs, got a job in a hospital (lasted a few days), got teaching jobs in a school, and worked at Donna Karan, schlepping clothes. Oh, I worked for David Paterson, who was our governor for some time . . . I worked for him (one summer) when he was running for public advocate, I did everything in that office.

Monte's work at ASCAP was from 1983 to part of 1985, but "I had to leave. I noticed that my skills were diminishing, I didn't have time to practice, working from 9 to5 was too much so I decided to go for this music thing, see what I could do. I knew the Marsalis brothers, Donald Harrison, and Terence Blanchard, who I knew from Berklee. They were all on Columbia Records."

Aaron Diehl

A thirty-two-year-old classically trained pianist and composer (who is also a licensed pilot), Aaron Diehl has made an indelible mark on the jazz world over the last fifteen years. He showed an affinity for early jazz and mid-twentieth-century "third-stream" music, but his latest evolution comes as he begins to tackle modern classical works, recently performing Gershwin with the New York Philharmonic, Cleveland Orchestra, and Los Angeles Philharmonic. Diehl has collaborated with living masters ranging from NEA Jazz Master Benny Golson to twentieth-century classical titan Philip Glass, while establishing himself as one of the preeminent interpreters of the Great American Songbook in his own trio and with the vocalist Cécile McLorin Salvant. Born in 1985 in Columbus, Ohio, to a funeral director and a former Olympian turned education administrator, Aaron Diehl grew up in a nurturing musical environment. His grandfather, Arthur Baskerville, a pianist and trombonist, was an early influence. He began studying classical piano at age seven, while his passion for jazz was further fueled while attending the Interlochen Arts Camp as a preteen, where he met the pianist Eldar, who exposed him to Oscar Peterson and Art Tatum recordings.

At age seventeen, Diehl was a finalist in Jazz at Lincoln Center's Essentially Ellington competition, where he was noticed by Wynton Marsalis. Soon after, Diehl was invited to tour Europe with the Wynton Marsalis Septet (Marsalis has famously referred to him as "The Real Diehl.") That fall, he would matriculate to the Juilliard School, studying with jazz pianists Kenny Barron and Eric Reed and classical pianist Oxana Yablonskaya. Diehl came to wider recognition in 2011 as winner of the American Pianists Association's Cole Porter Fellowship, which included $50,000 in career development and a recording contract with the esteemed Mack Avenue Records.

Aaron has been a staple of the New York jazz scene since 2007. His role as pianist and musical director for vocalist Cécile McLorin Salvant, the most arresting and authentic jazz vocalist to emerge in three decades, has enhanced his profile well beyond the jazz world. Diehl & Salvant's musical partnership is one of the most fruitful in recent memory.

www.aarondiehl.com

Tia Fuller

Tia grew up in suburbs of Colorado into a musical family: Dad played bass, Mom was a vocalist, her sister plays piano, and her little brother plays drums. Her parents started a group called "Fuller Sound" who gigged locally. And they listened to jazz all weekend! When it came time to choose a college, she decided to apply to Spelman College and not to Denver, where she could have gone tuition free. After watching the popular TV program *A Different World*, which was centered on a black college, she wanted to have the HBCU (Historically Black College and University) experience. Though Tia was in the drum corps, it was a dream of hers to play the saxophone, "I was at a crossroads after high school. I had a dream to play sax, but I knew that I had to get better at it. When I took it seriously I was a junior in college, I was eighteen at Spelman College, my freshmen year, and saw that there was no longevity in drum corps . . ." Spelman didn't have a music department, to speak of (there were only two other women studying music), so Tia took advantage of the burgeoning jazz scene in Atlanta by going to jam sessions and meeting the players on the scene: Terreon Gully, Russell Gunn, and other musicians.

I had goal points. I had read an article by Geri Allen in *DownBeat*—"Crystallized Vision." I knew I wanted to move to New York City but took a detour when I got my master's degree at Colorado–Boulder. I met Byron Stripling there, who asked us to visualize our future. The first exercise was to envision where we wanted to work, what the room looked like . . . second exercise was to write freely what we wanted to accomplish in the next ten years. I wrote down that I wanted to be a sidewoman, wanted to record, move to New York. . . . It was ten years later I saw what I had written and that I had hit 98 percent of those things listed. I knew I had a clear direction and the people I wanted to surround myself with; knew I wanted to be around abundance. And I'm blessed. I tell my students, "do the work and you'll be blessed with abundance too." Align yourself with the law of attraction, metaphysically speaking . . .

www.tiafuller.com

Allan Harris

Born in Brooklyn, New York, Allan Harris was surrounded by music throughout his childhood.

He moved from Brooklyn, New York, to Pittsburgh, Pennsylvania, where he got to know Joe Grushecky and play with several bands. His mother was a classical pianist, and his aunt was an opera singer who later turned to the blues. Because his Aunt Theodosia attracted the attention of famed music producer Clarence Williams (you know, the one who made Bessie Smith famous), he became a regular dinner guest and often brought along other performers such as Louis Armstrong. Armstrong once babysat young Harris and terrified him with his "froglike voice."

Although he grew up with music, it was not until he got to college that the "musician" seeds began to germinate within him. Not sure of the genre on which he should concentrate, he simply started going to clubs. When Allan sang in coffee shops, he started making money playing music.

> I played guitar first. I started to sing along when I started to play in bands. It was an ego thing. I could do singing a lot better than the leader. I noted the reaction of audiences to me versus him. Through that, I developed my voice and said, "I could do *this!*" I started making money playing music, so I knew that I could be good at this and have a voice in this where I could support myself. As I progressed in school, I went to jam sessions doing R&B and a few [jazz] standards.

Harris has thrilled audiences all over the world. He has performed for sold-out venues in Germany, at the Komische Opera House in Berlin, and with the New York Voices in Nuremberg. He has also performed with James Morrison for the television show *Swing It*; in a ten-day, standing-room-only tour of Israel; in the Espoo Jazz Festival in Finland; in Lugano, Switzerland, with Jon Faddis and the Big Band de Lausanne singing the lead in Duke Ellington's *Sacred Mass*; and at

Lincoln Center's new Rose Theater. The DVD recording of the performance in Lugano, Switzerland, has aired all over the country on public television and is available on both CD and DVD formats.

Since the first edition of this book, he says:

> It has been a roller-coaster ride but an exhilarating one to say the least. The musicians that I been working with since 2005 have been varied and very instrumental in getting my message across to my audiences. Some musicians can be, like myself, chameleons and can delve into my many projects with the spirit I need for that moment. Some are exact and perfect with a certain style and sound that only they can bring to the table. All in all, each phase of my career is reflected in the choice of artists that have lent their skill and their talent to me.

www.allanharris.com

Javon Jackson

Tenor saxophonist Javon Jackson came into international prominence touring and recording with the legendary drummer Art Blakey as a member of his band, Art Blakey and the Jazz Messengers. Symbolizing a new generation of musicians that blended tradition with neo-jazz, Jackson went on to release fourteen recordings as a band leader and tour and record over 135 CDs with jazz greats including Elvin Jones, Freddie Hubbard, Charlie Haden, Betty Carter, Cedar Walton, Ron Carter, Donald Byrd, Dr. Lonnie Smith, Richard Davis, Bobby Hutcherson, Curtis Fuller, Joanne Brackeen, Stanley Turrentine, and Ben E. King. In addition to his performance schedule, Javon Jackson is a highly sought-after jazz educator, conducting clinics and lectures at universities throughout the United States and abroad. He served as Assistant Professor of Jazz at Long Island University (1996–1998) and in the Conservatory of Music at Purchase College (1999–2007). In 2013, Javon accepted the position of director of the Jackie McLean Institute of Jazz at the University of Hartford.

He knew he wanted to be a jazz musician when he was a kid.

> My parents played lots of music in the house from the
> Four Tops to Miles Davis: black music. My dad's favor-
> ite musician was Gene Ammons, and I also heard Sonny
> Stitt and loved his playing, I was thirteen. . . . Stitt came
> to Denver, my dad took me backstage, I was thirteen and
> watched that first set and I said, "I'm gonna do just what he
> does, he travels the world, makes records and lives in New
> York City." Later I became aware of Art Blakey ("Bu") and
> Wynton Marsalis (he was in Art's band). My goal at sixteen
> was to play with Bu. I met Wynton's brother, Branford,
> later because I met (their other brother) Delfeayo, who
> was with me in an American marching band. We were
> marching and Wynton and Branford would came to see
> their baby brother. I got to be close with him. Branford
> came to visit and met my parents. He told my parents that
> it was a good idea for me to be a musician. I had a scholar-
> ship at Denver University, but after one semester I trans-
> ferred to Berklee. I got a gig working with Bu, thanks to
> Donald Brown. Mom wanted me to stay in school, but I
> told my mom I'd go back and get my degree. I couldn't do
> Bu and school, I failed . . .

With his sights set on the jazz mecca, New York City, Javon zeroed
in on a few musicians to meet.

> When I got to New York I looked at five people whose
> careers I respected: Jimmy Heath, Benny Golson, Ron
> Carter, Rufus Reid, and Kenny Barron. They were very
> successful, had families, teaching, looked like they had a
> nice lifestyle. I started to hang out with all of them. They
> helped me become the individual I am. Kenny is such a
> hard worker, dedicated, Benny is professional, Rufus, a
> good team player, and Barron is so consistent, and Heath

has simple, insightful knowledge. In their own way they don't put themselves about the music. Young people should remember no one person is bigger than the music and don't be afraid to ask questions, ask if you don't know. I've learned from so many people . . .

www.javonjackson.com

Mikael "Mika" Karlsson

Mikael Karlsson moved to New York City from Sweden in 2000 and graduated summa cum laude with departmental honors with a master's degree in classical composition from the Aaron Copland School of Music in 2005. Karlsson writes music ranging from modern ballets at major opera houses to chamber music, operas, and orchestral music. His music has been performed at Carnegie Hall, (Le) Poisson Rouge, Vienna State Opera, Lincoln Center, MoMA, the Ecstatic Music Festival, and the PROTOTYPE festival. His pieces with celebrated choreographer Alexander Ekman have premiered at the Royal Swedish Opera (*Midsummer Night's Dream*, 2015), the Oslo Opera (*A Swan Lake*, 2014), the Semperoper (*COW*, 2016), and the Paris Opera Ballet (*Play*, 2017). His many collaborators include ICE, ACME, Mivos Quartet, Claire Chase, Callie Day, Anna von Hausswolff, Lykke Li, Mariam Wallentin, Alicia Keys, and Lydia Lunch.

I decided to become a musician when I dropped out of law school at twenty-one, it was very late. But I was concerned that I couldn't make a living (as a musician, not as a lawyer). [He laughs.] I had fear of the business, itself, didn't know if I could turn it into a career. I never took being a musician seriously, found it interesting, listened to film composers. Had a few tools to see that I could turn it into a career. I was crazy about Michael Nyman, a film composer, and others. There was a different way [of composing] in Europe than in the states, not like John B.

Williams, they are more eighteenth-century, quiet pieces. . . . I went to China in 1997. Beijing, it was unbearably hot, so I put on Nyman [listened on headphones] so it became a bearable experience. I played pop piano before I quit law school. The hardest thing was my first lesson with a Latvian teacher. She put a Mozart sonata (I didn't know that existed) to read something and play it, I thought she was joking. I didn't have to learn meters in pop, no shape, so it was an excruciating hour that I couldn't get through the music. She was honest and said, "Come back next week. What do you want to do with this?". I said I wanted to write music. That was the first time I admitted to myself I wanted to do it. Then I started tinkering on the piano and would play my music for a friend who would give me a critique. I took lessons with her for three or four years. First time I voiced that wish to myself. I would record ten seconds on a tape recorder, I only had fragments, then I would play for my friend Pernilla. . . . I know how pop tunes went but didn't have to learn meters, key signatures, just saw the shape of that music so I figured it out. . . . I wrote for the process itself, I didn't know where that would lead me. I thought I would make an EP to hand to people.

To support himself, Mika took odd jobs. "I was working for a liquor store to pay for piano lessons. I was wasting time and money in law school . . ." He was passionate about music and knew he needed a change. His reason for moving to the United States was to attend a university that was dedicated to music.

In Sweden, all applications are centralized, and there was no way I'd get into a school there, only two spaces/positions for composition students at the Royal Academy of Music/year and I knew I'd never get it. My piano teacher suggested that I apply in the States, there were more positions and less expensive ones. Arizona lost my application; New York City seemed like an interesting place to become a new person. Starting at twenty-five I needed to go somewhere where people didn't know I was just starting. I got into Aaron Copland School of Music–Queens College. I was put in remedial theory because I didn't know anything (it was for my undergrad, it's easy to get in there but harder to stay).

www.mikaelk.com

Paula Kimper

Paula M. Kimper has been active in New York City for thirty-five years as a composer of opera, theater, dance, film, and song. Her first opera, *Patience & Sarah* (Lincoln Center Festival 1998), was commissioned and produced by American Opera Projects. *The Captivation of Eunice Williams* (Reid Theatre, Deerfield, Massachusetts, 2004) has been seen at The Smithsonian National Museum of the American Indian, in Washington, DC, and toured the Balkan region in 2008. *Truth: An American Opera About Sojourner Truth* (Academy of Music, Northampton, Massachusetts, 2012) appeared in the New York International Fringe Festival in 2013, and at Riverside Theatre inside Historic Riverside Church in 2014. She was one of five inaugural participants in the Columbia University Community Scholars Program. *"Here is a Place"* was commissioned by OPERA America for *The OPERA America Songbook* to commemorate the 2012 opening of the National Opera Center in New York City. *One Art* was commissioned by soprano Laure Meloy, who stars in the one-woman opera/cabaret based on Elizabeth Bishop's life and poetry. Paula Kimper Ensemble is sponsored by Fractured Atlas and is in the New York Opera Alliance. Her complete catalog can be found in the Loeb Music Library of Harvard University.

Before finding her way to opera, Paula Kimper came to New York City for a different musical experience:

I moved to New York City in 1979 and went into the pop-music field, into songwriting, and I had a small band for about five years where I wrote all the songs, but they never connected with a singer who could present them. I'm not a singer; I played piano. That evolved naturally into stuff, using a custom synthesizer in my own studio, and I could do it all by myself. That led me into film scoring and doing music for theater. Listen, you say you decide to change genres; I don't think of it as a decision *before* it happens, it is almost like it happens, then you decide to follow it. It feels like you are being shuttled through a process, then you never know where it will lead. While you are doing it, you just know it will lead somewhere, but I never thought I'd write an opera. I liked opera, and I listened to opera broadcasts, and I was in opera in college where they needed stage bands. I played in the orchestra, and I always thought it had too many notes, and I never thought that I could write all those notes, but I'm older. You really can sit longer, and things build up, and you can write all those notes.

www.paulakimper.com

Dorothy Lawson

Canadian-born cellist Dorothy Lawson comes from the world of classical orchestral and chamber music, with a doctorate from Juilliard, a career in Vienna, and performing experiences with such well-known musical organizations as the New York Philharmonic, the American Symphony, and the Orpheus Chamber Orchestra. In contrast, she performs regularly with modern-dance companies and figures such as Mikhail Baryshnikov and the White Oak Dance Project, as well as new music groups such as the Bang on a Can All-Stars. Lawson is a founding member of New York's premier new music string quartet, ETHEL.

"You pick it up [a musical instrument], and sooner or later, you've been doing it all of your life." Her story is not unusual. "I picked up the cello at age nine, not that young. For me, there was something healthy that it was a choice that I made." She knew right away that she wanted to be a classical musician.

> Classical music was the language in my household. My parents did not listen to popular music on the radio and never bought any. I grew up loving classical music, and then I was offered a chance at school. I was happy, and my parents were very excited. They did not push me. It just became part of my life and part of my sense of myself that I never considered giving it up. It was a very satisfying experience. I got good feedback from people, my teachers, and I was encouraged all the way along.

Being from Canada, Dorothy wanted to try her hand in the United States.

> I came to the States to go to Juilliard. Before coming, I had done an undergrad degree at Toronto, at the local university with a good music program. Then I chose to go to Vienna for three years to study with a great cello teacher there. When I came back to North America, I tried working in Toronto for about a year. Then I decided to see what the big deal was about at Juilliard.

www.ethelcentral.org

Ulysses Owens Jr.

An artist "who takes a backseat to no one"—the *New York Times*. This quote aptly represents the quality that has spearheaded his remarkable ascent as one of today's premier drummers, or perhaps his evolution as a producer, composer, educator, and entrepreneur. He has established himself as a leader in his generation of jazz artists, admired for his sensitive, fiery, and complex playing, vivid display of textural nuance, and gift for propelling a band with charisma and integrity.

Both humble in person and imposing behind a kit, he is a graduate of the inaugural Jazz Studies Program at the Juilliard School and a two-time Grammy Award winner, and he earned his stripes as a member of bassist Christian McBride's acclaimed trio and the driving force of McBride's big band.

Ulysses received his first Grammy in 2010 for his performance on Kurt Elling's *Dedicated To You* and his second Grammy for the Christian McBride Big Band album *The Good Feeling*. In addition to the two Grammy Awards, he has also received four Grammy nominations for his work with Christian McBride and Joey Alexander. Incredibly versatile, he has toured and recorded with artists including Wynton Marsalis, Kurt Elling, Diane Schuur, Renée Fleming, Monty Alexander, Russell Malone, and Mulgrew Miller. As a recording artist, Ulysses has released three albums of his own, beginning in 2009 with *It's Time for U*, which featured four original compositions and arrangements. His second album, *Unanimous*, was released on the European jazz label Criss Cross, and *Onward and Upward* was released in 2014 on the D-Clef Record Label. As coleader of New Century Jazz Quintet, he has released two albums with the Japanese record label Spice Of Life, *Time is Now* and *In Case You Missed Us*.

He began playing the drums at the age of two. In his younger years, he played many types of music, but for the most part, his musical experiences centered on the church. By the time he was in his early teens, he realized that he would become a jazz musician and received a full scholarship to study at the Juilliard School. There he began actively playing in the New York scene. While a student, he met Eric Reed, who hired him and showed him the ropes. He told Ulysses that he needed a plan and that "New York City is where you get in line and wait. It takes about five years to get beyond but don't give up. Save all of your money, take all gigs, get cheap rent, and hustle."

www.usojazzy.com

Jeremy Pelt

A graduate of Berklee School of Music, Pelt moved to New York City when he was twenty-one.

I didn't want to stay in Boston. New York City was the mecca of what I wanted to do, where the industry was that I was working hard to be in, it was a logical move. I decided to be a musician very early on, probably when I was 13, maybe earlier than that. I started playing trumpet a long time ago, I was two or three, I took a liking to it, long before I was expected to know what I wanted to do in life. . . . I was in classical music more than anything before jazz hit. I'd have conversations with myself and that I didn't care about not being a millionaire.

At Berklee, they had music business as one of the majors, but "I was a film scoring major. . . . My interests were to only play trumpet so I pursued film school as a day job while at night I worked on my craft—all four years."

His first few months, he struggled to find his way.

When I came to New York City I started from scratch, I did a day job. When you leave college and leave the security of the institution, you're faced with how am I going to live. I got to New York City in August of 1998. I had a little bit of money saved up, had money saved for rent (first and last), so I had to have roommates and I had $800 to move in and had to figure out how to scrounge for money to pay rent every month. I worried about how I was going to eat and pay rent and transportation every month. So I did what I had to do and worked at Sam Goody's.

All of his roommates were Berklee graduates.

Fortunately, the day job didn't last long; in April 1999, he quit. Those college years of hard work paid off because he had met people before his move who opened doors for him.

I have to say, looking back, what happens is that I even, in my last few years of college, would always come to New

York during spring breaks so I made connections with people that were very key. James Zollar was very important referring me to gigs, first a Ska band, the Skatalites, then I got a call to sit in with the Mingus Big Band, and Derrick Gardner helped get me work. When I moved here, Philip Harper was good about sending me to gigs he thought I could do. There was always waiting by the phone [for gigs], but back then that's what it was. I was somewhat aggressive, I'd go to jam sessions (they paid $30). I saw a sign, like the song "My Way," and I did it my way and didn't go to the "hot spots"; for me I was never comfortable where I'd immediately get challenged, I didn't want to handle the vibe from people, the in people . . . Cleo's was like Switzerland . . . Philip Harper gave me that gig. Eventually musicians would come through.

www.jeremypelt.net

Around 2000, Pelt worked with Louis Hayes; his stint with Eric Reed followed.

Eric Reed

Eric Reed joined Marsalis's Septet (1990–1991; 1992–1995). He also spent two years with the Lincoln Center Jazz Orchestra (1996–1998), making countless recordings and television appearances with them. Between 1991 and 1992, Reed worked in the bands of Freddie Hubbard and Joe Henderson. Though a leader, he continues to perform and record with an assorted multitude of masters, including Wayne Shorter, Ron Carter, Cassandra Wilson, Jimmy Heath, Clark Terry, Dianne Reeves, and a host of other diverse performers including Natalie Cole, Patti LaBelle, Oleta Adams, Edwin Hawkins, Jessye Norman, and Quincy Jones. Since 1995, Reed has been touring the world with his own ensembles, making serious waves in the jazz community.

Throughout the 2000s, Reed provided artistic direction for singers Paula West and Mary Stallings, for whom he produced 2013's *But*

Beautiful. "The art of accompanying singers has been ingrained in me since I was a child playing in church," he remarks. Under the auspices of the Juilliard School of Music, the New School, and Manhattan School of Music, Reed also began to teach privately and helped to direct young luminaries like Aaron Diehl and Kris Bowers toward paths that "might help enhance what they were already doing and get them to become more developed musicians. This is why I don't call myself a teacher, but a mentor."

There was no question that he would become a musician, though he had brief "day jobs" at A&M Records in 1987 and 1988. Much later, he worked as music director in a church, but it was in music.

> A day job one has to have, because music isn't [always] enough and not in your field. (Musicians job-shame you.) The gift of music was given to me by God. I probably always knew, but it did not manifest itself as a goal until I was a teenager. I think that everybody knows, everybody always knew. My talent was extraordinary for someone five years old; it was clear that this would not be a passing fancy. I played with other kids, but music was always the center. My childhood was typical, but more often than not, I was at the piano or listening to music. One of the earliest recordings of myself was at eleven to twelve years old at a church service. When I listen now, I say, "That was really good." If you listen to it, you can tell that it was something that a child would not play. A child sits at the piano and tends to bang out, but I was not doing that, it was by ear. Nobody taught me; that is why I knew it was a God-given talent. I could listen to a recording and hear what I heard, listen to a few bars, and I could play it.
>
> Our neighbors, Mack and Betty Hall, had a piano. The teacher did not drive, so he would come to their house on the bus, in Philadelphia, Pennsylvania. Mack was a good friend of jazz pianist Bobby Timmons. We did not get a piano until I was seven years old. SEPTA [the

public transportation system] went on strike, so that was the end of my lessons. We moved to a suburb in Philly called Bala Cynwyd, so I went to a music school there. The piano was a light lime green/yellow console. There was a mirror on it, the lid, so you could see your hands, and I thought that was kind of cool. Then I enrolled in the Settlement Music School; Christian McBride went there, Stanley Clarke, and Al Di Meola, too. When I was eleven, we moved to Los Angeles, and there I was able to get wider exposure to jazz. In Philly, I was in church doing gospel. The idea that there was a "scene" was unbeknownst to my parents and me. My parents did not listen to much jazz, so they weren't going to jazz clubs. I had heard some records, but most of my exposure was gospel music. My parents did not mind showing me off, but they were not backstage parents; in fact, they tried to play it down, so I would not get a big head. . . . It was not until 1985, when I met the Clayton Brothers, John and Jeff, Gerald Wilson, Clora Bryant, while I was living in Los Angeles, that I figured I could do this for a living. I had no idea what I was going to do. Word began to spread that there was a young kid who could play jazz piano. I went to the Colburn Community School of Performing Arts, an annex of University of Southern California (USC). My theory instructor, Jeff Lavner, knew that I liked jazz and made me tapes. He went to the dean of the school and urged him to do something for me. There was also another kid, Myron McKinley, one year older than me, also black; we were the "two spots." They were more than happy to take advantage of this interesting opportunity, so they decided to send us out to other schools. This was good exposure for the school, these two kids who played jazz. We would talk about the music we were doing, that was before Wynton Marsalis. I think that Jeff Lavner did not get the recognition that he should have gotten, and Joe Thayer, of course. Joe knew

Wynton when he was a teenager. So he called Wynton and told him that he needed to hear Myron and me. Wynton came out to Los Angeles once or twice a year to play at the now-defunct Westwood Playhouse, so he came and gave us a master class. Wynton had won two Grammys, I taped the class, I tape everything, and Wynton was impressed with me. I had played some Tatum stuff. He took more interest in me than Myron; I guess Wynton saw in me my passion.

www.ericreed.net

Bobby Sanabria

Bobby Sanabria is a seven-time Grammy nominee as a leader. He is a noted drummer, percussionist, composer, arranger, conductor, producer, educator, documentary filmmaker, and bandleader of Puerto Rican descent born and raised in New York's South Bronx. He was the drummer for the acknowledged creator of Afro-Cuban jazz, Mario Bauzá, touring and recording three CDs with him, two of which were Grammy nominated, as well as an incredible variety of artists. From Dizzy Gillespie, Tito Puente, Mongo Santamaria (with whom he started his career) Paquito D'Rivera, Yomo Toro, Candido, The Mills Brothers, Ray Barretto, Chico O'Farrill, Francisco Aguabella, Henry Threadgill, Luis "Perico" Ortiz, Daniel Ponce, Larry Harlow, Daniel Santos, Celia Cruz, Adalberto Santiago, Omara Portuondo, Pedrito Martinez, Roswell Rudd, Patato, David Amram, the Cleveland Jazz Orchestra, Michael Gibbs, Charles McPherson, Jon Faddis, Bob Mintzer, Phil Wilson, Randy Brecker, Charles Tolliver, M'BOOM, Michelle Shocked, Marco Rizo, and many more. In addition, he has guest-conducted and performed as a soloist with numerous orchestras like the WDR Big Band, the Airmen of Note, the U.S. Jazz Ambassadors, the University of Wisconsin–Eau Claire Big Band, and the University of Calgary Big Band, to name just a few.

His latest recording, released in July 2018, is a monumental Latin jazz reworking of the entire score of *West Side Story* entitled *West Side Story Reimagined*, on the Jazzheads label in celebration of the show's recent sixtieth anniversary (2017) and the centennial of its composer, Maestro Leonard Bernstein (2018). Partial proceeds from the sale of this historic double-CD set go the Jazz Foundation of America's Puerto Relief Fund to aid Bobby's ancestral homeland after the devastation from hurricanes Irma and Maria. He was nominated for a Grammy for *West Side Story Reimagined*.

Bobby Sanabria said,

> When I was twelve years old, Tito Puente and Machito and others came to perform, and I watched them from my neighbor's bedroom. I urged him to go down to see it, and we got there when Tito took a solo. I was mesmerized, and it was like an epiphany, and I knew I wanted to do it the rest of my life. I started working when I went to Berklee College of Music. My father was so busy, and he had gotten laid off when the Vietnam War ended, and he could not take the long travel. We were on welfare for a year, and it was embarrassing. When I told my father that he had to sign the papers for me to get a loan for school, and I told him I was going to do music, he said that he thought it was a hobby, and he freaked out. My mother made him sign the papers. In high school, I had started my group, Ascension, but I had no real musical knowledge. In that first incarnation, I was writing arrangements and melded all the aesthetics I was acquiring. Berklee was an incredible experience for me, but it was very difficult. My first year I took applied music, the hardest program at the school. My first year in Boston, I got a reputation. No one there was into Latin music at all.

www.bobbysanabria.com.

Richard Smallwood

Richard Smallwood was a child prodigy, a baby in the crib making music. Never one to doubt his calling or his choice of genre, he says,

As far back as I remember, as long as I was aware of being alive, I wanted to be a musician. I showed musical talent before I began to talk. I would hum melodies I had heard at church; it freaked my mother out. My parents put a toy piano in the crib; I'd sit up and bang rhythms on the keyboard. At five years of age, I started singing and playing by ear. By the time I was seven, I was playing in my dad's church. I've never wanted to do anything else. Music has always been one of the most important things in my life. I didn't know that I would be successful.

I asked him when he knew he would be a professional musician. "When I was in college at Howard University in DC, I was part of the first gospel group on the Howard campus called the Celestials. Donny Hathaway was one of the organ and keyboard players and singers. When he left, I stepped into his place."

These sources of inspiration include Roberta Flack (his teacher), Aretha Franklin, the Hawkins Family, and Kathleen Battle. A world-class composer, pianist, and arranger, Smallwood has clearly and solidly changed the face of gospel music. He can impeccably blend classical movements with traditional gospel and arrive at a mix that is invariably Smallwood's alone. A diverse and innovative artist, Smallwood has achieved many honors; Dove Awards and a Grammy also attest to his talents. Richard's music has never been confined to any one artistic genre. His song "I Love the Lord" crossed onto the big screen when Whitney Houston sang it in the film *The Preacher's Wife*. R&B artists Boyz II Men used the same song in the tune "Dear God" on their CD *Evolution*.

Camille Thurman

Acclaimed by *DownBeat* as a "rising star" singer with "soulful inflection and remarkable, Fitzgerald-esque scat prowess" and hailed by *All About Jazz* as a "first class saxophonist that blows the proverbial roof off the place." Camille Thurman has been amazing audiences throughout the world with her impeccable sound, remarkable vocal virtuosity, and captivating artistry. Many have compared her vocal abilities to the likes of Ella Fitzgerald and Betty Carter. Her lush, rich, and warm sound on the tenor saxophone has led others to compare her to tenor greats Joe Henderson and Dexter Gordon.

She was raised in St. Albans, Queens, where many great musicians lived, including Ella Fitzgerald, Count Basie, Illinois Jacquet, Louis Armstrong, and Duke Ellington. While her mother was getting her degrees—one was a master's in reading and literacy—she did her thesis on storytelling and was able to make a connection between those musicians, music, and reading.

Mom played a lot of their music, I was there with her soaking it up like a sponge. She also took me to see concerts. Music was taken out of the schools, so she sent me out of my neighborhood to a school up north that had a music program. The band teacher, Peter Archer, saw that I wanted to play something. He wanted to put me on trombone (said the trumpet would mess up my lips). I tried for one week but I hated it. When I told him that I wanted to play flute, he said "no" because there were too many flute players. Determined, I was able to get a flute because a woman in church had broken up with a musician who'd left all of his instruments in her garage, so she gave me his flute. My mom had confiscated a mouthpiece from one of her students that I thought was for the clarinet. I took it to school, showed Mr. Archer, who said that it was for the saxophone but that he didn't think I would learn, he wanted me to stick with the flute. I cut a deal with him that I'd study the sax during lunch; he agreed. So, I taught myself a few things, it was then that he knew that I was serious. He said I needed to go to the Fiorello H. LaGuardia High School of Music & Art and Performing Arts. (I'd never heard of that school.) He took me there for a jazz concert. (Bob Stewart was a teacher.) First time I saw girls in the section, Lakecia Benjamin was one. I auditioned and got it. It was Sarah Vaughan and Dexter Gordon that I wanted to tap into musically. Dexter's sound was huge! I was thirteen, the horn was as big as me, I wanted to be six feet tall on my horn.

What began as a promising musical endeavor turned out to be a demoralizing experience for Camille. "At LaGuardia I had a hard time, the first two years were great because Bob got us excited about the music and the history. The last two years were rough because Bob left and the guys (male students) let us know that they didn't want us (girls) there. Bob had been able to keep everyone in check." Having internalized the negativity and belief that she couldn't play, her senior year she got depressed and disappointed and lost her desire to play. She'd had enough of the sexism and switched to geology but couldn't get money for the schools she wanted to attend. Having fallen in love with the sciences, Camille went to Binghamton University for science. A music teacher saw that she played an instrument and encouraged her to audition for the band. Filled with self-doubt, she believed that she wasn't good and decided to not try out; she was traumatized. Instead, the teacher asked her to go to the audition and take an improv class. That's where he heard that she could *really* play!

> He asked me to join the band, which was great. I wasn't judged or criticized. And, I met New York City musicians who came to play. It was there that I met Tia Fuller, who was touring with Beyoncé then. I'd never seen a woman playing like that. Tia showed me that you can sound great, you can be a woman, and you can play. I made my decision to be a musician but my parents were concerned about how I would make a living. When I graduated, I gave my diploma to my parents.

www.camillethurmanmusic.com

Michael Wolff

Michael Wolff seemed to always know that he would be a musician.

I guess the reason why I never even thought about it is because my father was an amateur musician. He grew up in Indianola, Mississippi, so he grew up in the same town as B. B. King, Albert King, and Muddy Waters, those guys. He played as a kid in the band with a saxophone player by the name of Blue Mar. I grew up in New Orleans. My dad, from the time I was growing up, played his favorites, Sinatra, George Shearing, Oscar Peterson, Ray Charles, and folks like that. Count Basie was his favorite big band. He'd sit me down when I was a real little boy, I'd remember listening to a segue and he'd say, "See what's happening on the music, you got to pay attention," and he'd try to explain it to me. So I just grew up hearing that kind of music and having that kind of blues underneath. When I started playing music, I had that kind of . . . I grew up in the sixties and seventies with the Beatles, the rock and roll, and all that, I played the drums and all that, but when I played the piano, which was my instrument, it seemed like that is what came out, so that's what I was drawn to.

I knew when I wanted to be a professional musician—when I was in high school, I was fifteen, tenth grade—and that's when I didn't even consider anything else. I always loved it; my parents said, "You want to play jazz, you have to take classical piano lessons until you are thirteen to fourteen." So I did that, but I just wanted to do jazz; I always did jazz on the side. When I got to be fifteen, I got out of tenth grade—by then we moved to Berkeley, California, in the late sixties [sighs]—what a different world. But then I had a great jazz piano teacher, Dick Whittington; it just was like coming home.

Wolff's entry into a pan-global mix of sounds was triggered by a trip that his parents took to Yemen and Ethiopia. As he explains,

> They brought me back a bag of cassettes to check out, music that they had gathered from their travels. The tapes were all labeled in Arabic, so I didn't know what they really were. It was a mixture of African sounds and Indian beats that was absolutely amazing. Those countries have somehow absorbed that influence of tablas and tamboura . . . that kind of drone built into their musical culture . . . along with the influence of African percussion. To me, that was really the essence of what Miles was trying to get to with *On the Corner*. All this music, harmonically, is so simple. But the intrigue comes from the groove, the textures and tension in the music. I never really liked the pyrotechnical kind of chops-oriented fusion stuff. That's not what I want to play. I want the music to flow and breathe more. And I just love the aspect of mixing different elements together in the music.

www.michaelwolff.com

NOTES

- Follow your passion.
- Study.
- Develop a plan.
- Be determined and flexible. Fine-tune your plan as you move along.
- It's OK to take a "day job" when necessary.

CHAPTER 2
Learning One's Craft

Musicians learn their craft in myriad ways. It can be from listening to records, by taking classes, studying with mentors, or working in varied musical situations. Kenny Washington advises,

> It is important to tell musicians: Study the music, get a good teacher, listen to the musicians and players that came before you. Never let anyone tell you it's old-fashioned. Don't be afraid to copy any of the musicians. You must sound like others before you sound like yourself. In classical music, you have to go back; in jazz, the young people don't know nearly as much as they should about this music, and it's a disgrace. Learn standards; when the record company drops you, you'll have to be a sideman.

Unfortunately, this lack of historical curiosity among young musicians is as alarming in 2019 as it was when the first edition of this book was written. In 2002, a young jazz musician, a tenor saxophonist, asked a veteran musician why he needed to learn standards, songs that have become the canon of jazz. The veteran musician told him that one day that attitude would get him in trouble. As it turned out, about a year later, the two worked together on a date with Eric Reed. I was in the greenroom when Eric was going over the set. One of the tunes that Eric wanted to play was "Polka Dots and Moonbeams." The gentleman knew the song but only in *one* key, and it was not the key that Eric wanted to play. The young man took a few moments to practice the song, but on the stage, he struggled with it, and the others just played over him. Eric and I discussed his performance, and he replied, "I was shocked! How do you only know a song in one key? That's like only being able to make love in one position. I was pissed off at how he messed up some other tunes on the gig—he couldn't even hear what key we were in on some of the standards!" I asked Eric if he had known ahead of time of this musician's lack of knowledge of standards. Eric said, "Well, I wasn't too concerned because I had charts, but for cryin' out loud . . ." To that point, Michael Wolff learned early on from Cannonball Adderley that he should "learn everything in all keys and to play all over the keyboard." He "listened to the records and learned every tune."

For many years, Bobby Sanabria has been teaching on the college level and is very critical of today's students and their lack of curiosity about the music and the business. When he was coming of age, work was plentiful, especially in the Latin jazz scene. Now, not so much.

> I tell young people, you want to be a musician? Do you know the commitment to learn your craft? To have as many opportunities available to you? In the old days there was so much work, you could be mediocre and get a gig, then you'd get better. You'd take private lessons to get better. Today you don't have that anymore. For example, I tell the brass players if it was forty years ago you'd want to leave class early to do a salsa gig somewhere. . . . In the past students were working while in school and asked to leave early. They were all working. They weren't making lots of money, but they were working. They'd learn the ins and outs in the business, maybe even work in brutal

conditions. You have to learn as much of your craft and learn about being a professional in the business. Show up on time, dress properly, don't ask dumb questions or ask stupid things (like I don't have a tie, or a suit, do you have?). Don't be arrogant! The world owes you nothing. Follow the leader. Do what the gig calls for. Actress Lauren Bacall learned that the world doesn't owe you a damn thing. Can you play the heck out of your horn? Can you do the job and do it professionally? Do you know different styles of music? Can you play funk? Can you get into the band? Or do you say you don't do this or that, like dance? Dance is part of the tradition! All funk, R&B . . . and do you know how to say the two most important words, "thank you"? Do you say, "I can't do the job, but thank you for calling me . . ."? When they leave school, they have to know this. Luck plays a big role in the business. They have to be prepared for luck and have to deliver. They may not be doing their favorite kind of music, but if you get called for funk on the weekends, you better be able to throw down some funk.

FIND YOUR VOICE—DEVELOP YOUR OWN SOUND!

It is frustrating to hear terrific musicians whose sound I cannot identify. Think about this: can you hear the difference between Aretha Franklin and Beyoncé, Kem and Gregory Porter, John Coltrane and Stanley Turrentine and Miles Davis and Roy Hargrove? I venture to think that you might (though maybe not Roy Hargrove). Music schools are graduating more students at a faster rate than in years past. In this changing economy, competition for work is steep, and that is why it is in your best interest to learn your craft, develop your sound, and set yourself apart from your fellow musicians. I find it troubling that young musicians are starting to sound the same. Their musicianship is at a high level. Being "bland" works well in an ensemble setting and may be accepted as a leader. The problem is, the music is starting to sound the same.

If you are good at what you do, people will hear about you via word of mouth. In order to learn your craft, you must, of course, study, practice, and find places to work. Seek advice from those you respect. Watch what they do and glean the information that you need to advance your career. Natural ability alone is not enough for you to be a complete musician. One of the best methods to develop your voice is to start by copying musicians that you like, or want to sound like. Study their form, their licks, their phrasing. Take that information and incorporate your voice. Recently I read a short interview by Herbie Hancock where he cautioned musicians to *not* try to sound like *him*! There's only one Herbie, one Chick Corea, etc. To quote a line in the Billie Holiday song "God Bless the Child," "take what you need and leave the rest."

When Allan Harris started out, he understood what he needed to do to learn his craft:

> As I progressed in school, I went to jam sessions doing R&B and a few [jazz] standards. What helped me grow as an artist was jazz because of the melodies and you had to study your craft. . . . In jazz, because of the caliber of musicians I needed to play with and to accept me, I had to learn my craft, or I would not work with them. In other genres, the door was open. You had to have a certain look, some sort of gimmick, or fill the bill of what they were looking for that evening. In jazz it did not matter how; you had to learn your craft. You had to know the songs that were presented to you, and that was your calling card. I found that my participation was remunerated, not by the pay scale, but by growth. The more I learned the music, the more I grew as an individual.

Though he primarily considers himself to be a jazz musician, Jeff Clayton straddled genres. Because he knows so much music, he is comfortable in most settings.

I began in jazz music; it is the art of being a chameleon, it is so special, it prepares you to do any music. You steal solos, jazz, funk, or classical music; you just copy and mimic that. Then you understand the parameters of these styles, and good jazz musicians can copy. I started out on Concord Records as a jazz artist, then I did pop because someone asked me if I could, so I stole some solos, learned some songs of Stevie Wonder from his records until I knew how to play pop. When I did that, I changed the way I played in my mind and body and played pop. When I stopped playing pop, I turned on jazz and classical; they are closely related.

Both jazz and classical musicians tend to be highly trained, though there was a period where classical musicians looked down on jazz musicians because, as Bobby Sanabria stated, "Classical folks used to complain about jazz. They'd say, '[Musicians] they can't read music, they can't play the parts as written, jazz musicians' technique sucks, they play out of tune, not on the beat, etc.' I say they're wrong, because jazz musicians can play everything. Most jazz musicians are classically trained, as are most Latin musicians." In his nascent years, Eric Reed observed that the demands on a jazz musician can be at least as rigorous as those put upon a classical musician.

It was so bizarre, I'd be competing in jazz against classical [musicians]. There were music competitions; nobody was playing jazz, just me! I was the only one doing jazz. I was better than them; I played my music better than they played their music. I'd have my suit and tie, and I'd play with a lot of personality. Before people heard me play, they'd be intrigued by this thirteen- or fourteen-year-old kid who could articulate a point of view about music so eloquently. . . . Jazz and classical music are different types of music, but they both require a higher level of skill and discipline than most other types of music. Not to say that other music such as pop, R&B, doesn't require talent. What it takes to play both jazz and classical as a pianist is advance knowledge of all elements of music, melody, rhythm, and harmony, whereas in popular music, that level of skill is not required. That's why it's popular music. In pop music, you don't have to do a whole lot of things in order to appreciate it. It's designed for a certain kind of stimulation, whether it's emotional, mental, or mental de-stimulation. You don't have to know how to play the Rach 3—Rachmaninoff's Third Piano Concerto—to play pop music.

One cannot overestimate the importance of having or being a mentor. Eric Reed understands that.

I love teaching. I'm a player who teaches, not the reverse. There are students who get to college and don't know the rudiments, and I'll teach them. We are coming into a generation of young people who are further and further removed from the essential reference points that they need. I was lucky. I grew up in the last golden age of radio. Kids today just know one style of music, and if they get into jazz, *by luck*, they got it in high school or had a parent who was into jazz. We have more technically gifted players, but they lack arenas to gain life experience that will give them the street knowledge that you can get by playing with older cats who will talk to you when you do something wrong. The highest compliment in jazz is "[You] sound good."

Be versatile! I remember the first time I went to hear Ron Carter's Nonet and how surprised I was to see my friend the cellist Dorothy Lawson in the ensemble. Her classical training gave her the skills needed. She spent many years studying and understood the importance of surrounding herself with masters.

I spent a long time working with powerful people and being an apprentice and doing what they asked me to do or what they approved of. It never stopped me from feeling I had my own taste somewhere. The process for me to find my own voice was, for me, getting really secure and comfortable with the idea that I was going to say something without the approval of others and take the consequences.

CRAFT VERSUS ARTISTRY

Remember, there is a difference between learning your instrument and becoming a musician. Dorothy Lawson shares how she learned the distinction:

> From André Navarra, the teacher I studied with in Vienna. One thing he said in class stuck with me. He was very methodical, and he had a careful routine that he wanted us to follow, and if he felt someone was slacking off or doing something in more free form, he would say (in French), "Oh, yes, *you* are the artist; *I'm* just the craftsperson." In a way, it's cynical. It is good to be reminded that doing something well is important, no matter how "artistic" you think you are.

NOTES

- Study, practice, study.
- Seek mentors.
- Be honest with yourself about your musicianship.
- Have a plan: short and long range.

CHAPTER 3
Formal Education versus Learning Onstage

In 2000, I was asked to work with Ricky Minor, then-music director of BET's *Harlem Block Party*, when they were opening an office in New York City. The celebration was an evening of stars from all genres of black music: Stevie Wonder, Mary J. Blige, Wyclef Jean, and many others. During a rehearsal, one of the featured artists, a singer, came late, and she had not learned the song that she was supposed to sing (it was the Roberta Flack/Donny Hathaway duet, "Back Together"). I was sent to purchase the CD of the original recording so she and the band could learn it (they, too, had no knowledge of the song). After several listens to the song and several takes, she gave up and left the studio in disgust. Interesting, two of the other musicians in the house band could not "hear" their parts, either. During a break, I talked to the de facto band leader about the rehearsal and how difficult it was for him to work with them. He was a Berklee College graduate (whom I had met years earlier when he was playing jazz) who had left jazz to go to work with pop artists, including Madonna. He shared, with me, his frustration and that he had suggested that they should get some formal education. That night, the singer called Ricky and convinced him to let her sing *her* hit song, which he agreed, so the program was altered. In fairness to those musicians, in 2000 there was plenty of work across all platforms, so school was not as necessary.

Bill Zuckerman, founder of Music School Central, a music college student admissions advising firm, wrote a piece titled "What Happens to Music Majors After They Graduate College? New Study Reveals Amazing Data." He summarized and commented on a study by an accomplished and published music education professor at Indiana University, Peter Miksza, in conjunction with educator Lauren Hime during the years from 2012–2015 that tracked those who graduated with music degrees.[1]

Here are some excerpts from Zuckerman's piece:[2]

> If you aren't sure what the difference is, Music Education students are primarily trained to teach in the public school system, although many end up going into careers that include private school teaching and conducting regional youth ensembles.
>
> Music Performance majors, on the other hand, are those that majored in a specific instrument, usually in classical or jazz disciplines, although popular music and even hip-hop have now become majors at some colleges. [. . .]
>
> For the study, Peter & Lauren surveyed musicians from over 150 different institutions to ensure that not all of the results came from just a few schools.
>
> They surveyed high school, undergraduate, and graduate alumni for this piece. Overall, there were 1,434 respondents from liberal arts colleges, public and private universities, and institutions dedicated solely to the performing arts.

1   Peter Miksza and Lauren Hime, "Undergraduate Music Program Alumni's Career Path, Retrospective Institutional Satisfaction, and Financial Status," *Arts Education Policy Review* 116, no. 4 (2015): 1–13, doi: 10.1080/10632913.2014.945628.

2   Bill Zuckerman, "What Happens to Music Majors after They Graduate College? New Study Reveals Amazing Data," *Music School Central*, March 1, 2016, https://musicschool central.com/what-happens-to-music-majors-after-they-graduate-college-new-study -reveals-amazing-data/.

One thing to note is that the study only used respondents from US music schools. [. . .]

The Results of Peter & Lauren's Study

According to this study, over 50 percent of the students in the music performance group found work relevant to their major within four months of graduation.

Additionally, more than 75 percent of the music education group also found work within four months of graduation.

Ultimately, more than one out of every two of all the respondents stated that performance or education was their jobs. [. . .]

To put this in perspective, approximately one in four students who graduate college in other majors end up working in a field related to their major.

Another interesting thing to note is that one out of five in the performance group found a job concurrently teaching in a public school, suggesting that it is a relatively common practice for students who major in performance to also teach.

Those in the music education group reported annual incomes between $20,000 and $60,000, with a small number making over $60,000. The authors noted that although the average in this group would be lower than the national average salary of $56,000 for music education teachers, he concluded most musicians wouldn't attain the average salary until they are further along into their careers.

For music performance majors, the salaries were wider in range—although many reported starting annual incomes in the $20,000 area, some did make more than $60,000. [. . .]

Heck, I [Zuckerman] went to university for composition and am now a college consultant for music students looking to attain a degree in music. It took me years to get to where I am now, but I am here now and I am doing well. [...]

What about Musicians Outside of Performance and Teaching?

Although the study did not address majors outside of performance and teaching, the career prospects for those in other fields, such as Music Production and Music Composition, can be very good.

I [Zuckerman] have known composition alumni to make great salaries outside of teaching. The opportunities for composers includes, but is certainly not limited to, commissions for orchestral, chamber, and solo music, orchestration and arranging for other composers, engraving music (the art of taking written music and processing it through a notation program like Finale or Sibelius), writing film/commercial music, etc.

Music Production majors also have very good career prospects. Some of these include working in recording studios, working independently as recording engineers, mixing and mastering tracks and albums for artists, running live sound in music venues, producing & DJing music, and consulting for record labels. [...]

If you have a dream, a passion, and you desire to work in music, then even if you decide to regard any study, you can make a career for yourself after you graduate college.

The above study reveals some benefits to getting a degree in music. Music schools can provide the necessary experiences and training to help you navigate the industry. Colleges and universities offer an array of degrees from film scoring to engineering. (Will Calhoun and Jeremy Pelt, respectively, studied those at Berklee.) Higher education gives you exposure to your future peers and to some of the greatest leaders in your field. It will also give you discipline and structure. Another key element in acquiring a music education is the relationship that you build with your instructors. When doing your research into the institutions, look at the faculty list as well as the alumni. By the time you reach high school, determine if college is in your future. There are many schools with music programs, but few have highly developed, prestigious music programs. Tuition costs vary from as low as $12,000 to $60,000 per year. Do your homework to find what school is best for you.

Below are the top schools, worldwide, found on several lists:

- The Juilliard School
- Berklee College of Music
- Eastman School of Music
- University of Southern California Thornton School of Music
- Manhattan School of Music
- University of Music and Performing Arts, Vienna
- New England Conservatory of Music
- Yale School of Music
- Curtis Institute of Music
- The Royal Academy of Music
- Jacobs School of Music at Indiana University
- Mannes School of Music
- Oberlin Conservatory of Music
- Peabody Institute
- University of Miami Frost School of Music

THE PROS AND CONS OF GETTING A DEGREE

Some of the greatest jazz musicians could not read a lick of music, but their musicianship was, and is, beyond reproach. As in any art form, exceptions find their way to the top. The late Ruth Brown said,

> I had no formal training, and I can't read music. I could sing anything I heard. My music teacher in high school, Ora Lee Churchill, told me, "You're gonna regret that one

of these days." Sometimes when I went into the studio to record, the arranger would bring lead sheets. In the beginning, you did not have to worry about it; they'd send you a demo, and you would learn from the record. Now all of the arrangements have a sheet for vocal line, but I still can't read it; I hear it. I'm not sure that young people are really learning music now. They can make a star out of the mixing board. Anyone can sound like they are singing. In those days, that was impossible. One thing that was important was all of the *great* singers—Ella, Sarah, Carmen, Dinah—played piano. I didn't do any of that. Dizzy Gillespie said, "Ruth could hear a rat peeing in cotton because she can hear it." That is what I depended on. I can hear chord changes. That is why most of my musicians stayed with me.

According to Aaron Diehl, "education is important in anything, yes, recordings are still important to listen to but there are fewer opportunities to learn on the bandstand and why young people are creating opportunities for themselves." Ulysses Owens, who acquired his BA degree at the Juilliard School, said that "one doesn't need school to be a professional musician, education gives you a perspective yet you need to be focused on what you want to do as a performing artist. The top five jazz schools give you a network and you'll be learning and working with the best."

Richard Smallwood, who holds an MA from Howard University, supports that idea,

I think that it [formal education] is very important. If God has given us a gift, we are charged to develop it, and to be the best we can be. A lot of things that you know by ear, or that you do naturally, you get to understand why they are, or how they are put together. You learn about the history of music and why you do what you do. Knowing who the pioneers are helps you to be the best when you get there. I started formal classes at age seven and continued through until I graduated from Howard.

Some formal training is good, but work experience is invaluable. Ron Carter, an educator, suggests that on-the-job training is important:

Probably 60/40, sixty learning on the bandstand, forty meaning formal education. You can't have one successfully, completely, without the other. I mean, you need discipline to know how to prepare a lesson, how to prepare an arrangement. Discipline to learn how to arrange, how to compose. Bandstand: how to put two sides (sets) together and see what level your talent is. Yes, I worked as a musician while going to school.

Getting an advanced degree was one of the best decisions Javon Jackson made. While a student at Berklee College, he landed a dream gig when he joined the band of drummer Elvin Jones. Against his family's wishes, he dropped out of school to take that gig because that was an opportunity he wouldn't pass up—especially given the low band turnover—to play with those master musicians. After his stint with Elvin, he went on the road with trumpeter Freddie Hubbard. In 2003, while teaching at SUNY Purchase, upon the urging of the dean, Javon decided to complete his degree work. Along the way, Javon became friends with Ron Carter, who encouraged him to continue his education to seek an MA. Being armed with a bachelor's degree in music from the Berklee College of Music (Boston, Massachusetts) and a master's degree in music from Purchase College (Harrison, New York) put him on a trajectory that led him to his current position as professor and division director at the Jackie McLean Jazz Studies Division at the University of Hartford's Hartt School. The demands of academia have not diminished his recording and touring career; he has maintained his presence in both.

In spite of himself, Will Calhoun attended Berklee College. College wasn't something that he wanted to pursue, but he felt that he had no choice. In his junior year, he dropped out of school, but on the urging of Harry Belafonte and a promise of a gig upon graduation, he returned to finish his last year. Will explained that the upside to going to Berklee was that

> it benefited me because I was arrogant being up there, I hated Boston. I didn't want to go to college, my friends were starting to take off, Scott La Rock was the DJ and rapper with KRS-One, he was in my high school. He got a record deal and I was in the dorm eating Chinese food. . . . I was frustrated, I'd call home and saw that "my boys" were getting signed. Drummers I was study-ing, me, Sterling Campbell, and others were disciples of Kenwood Dennard. . . . I'd turn on the TV at night and would see, on the Johnny Carson show, my friends playing with Cyndi Lauper or Duran Duran, they were getting all of the great gigs. I was angry and bitter about being up there because I thought I was missing out on something. [Jazz master] Lou Donaldson is a mem-ber of my mother's church. My mother told him that I was a musician and that I wanted to go to school. She introduced me to Mr. Donaldson, I told him that I was studying with Horace Arnold and I was going to Berklee. He said, "What the hell you want to do that for?" Ralph MacDonald lived near us, I was a close friend with his son . . . Ralph said, "Calhoun, you're not gonna learn how to play in school, they'll turn you into one of the cookies . . ." But the hip-hop cats were encouraging me to go. They said, "naw, man, go up there and get that information, we need soldiers in other places . . ."

"It's difficult to tell your mother, who has two master's degrees and a PhD, that you don't want to go to school, so I had to find a way to make it work." He went to audition for New York University (where his mother and sister had received their master's degrees) but, instead, got directed to Berklee by Abdul Malik, an instructor in the NYU music department. The first year at Berklee was great.

> I thought that I'd learn how to play, they had some great instructors and students. . . . After the first year I realized that I wouldn't make it in the school as a performance major, the baddest cats were in New York who I could study with, so I switched my major to recording and engineering. That's how I benefited from the school but I still did my drumming. . . . I also took a film scoring class. All three years I was there I recorded my band, Dark Sarcasm. There I learned all of the components of recording. . . . It was a great incubator for me to get my act together, for me to realize my competition and the things I wasn't learning in New York City. . . . It was a great terrain for me to check myself.

Now an assistant professor at Michigan State University College of Music, Etienne Charles says,

> Formal education is learning your instrument, it doesn't have to be in a school. You can develop ensemble skills, but for jazz, [learning] on the bandstand is crucial, as is being onstage; you have to be in front of people. Universities should do more to create working and performing opportunities for students . . . they need to create steady work for them, not just one hits.

He was fortunate to attend a school that had great instructors, who included visiting musicians such as Marcus Roberts. "At Florida State the big band study was important but they emphasized more small combos group playing. Our combo class was important. Rodney Jordan had us learn music as a band. He had us learning from records for us to get a feel for how a band worked, then he would have us play the music that music."

As an instructor at Berklee College, Tia Fuller has an opportunity to steer students to develop a positive working mind-set beyond the academics. "How students talk to elders is embarrassing," she sighed. "They don't want to take a gig unless they're getting paid and they're in school! You never know what you'll learn by taking a free gig. It's a general narrative at the college because it's more performance oriented. If a professor is asking you to play with them you don't know what they have in mind for you. It's not about getting *paid*. They may be looking at how responsible you are, if you come to class on time . . ."

Tia Fuller and Camille Thurman did not attend the traditional jazz-oriented colleges, so the bulk of their knowledge was not necessarily garnered from school. Tia got her BA degree in music from Spelman College in Atlanta, Georgia (magna cum laude), and her master's degree in jazz pedagogy and performance from the University of Colorado at Boulder (summa cum laude). In graduate school, she was a teacher's assistant in a new program of theirs where she taught jazz improvisation. She also did her residency in the public school system.

After her bad experience at famed Fiorello H. LaGuardia High School of Music & Art and Performing Arts, Camille Thurman became sour on being a musician. In her senior year, she took off a semester and studied geology and fell in love with it. She was not in a financial position to attend the schools that she wanted, then set her sights to upstate New York for school. Determined to *not* do music, she attended Binghamton University, from which she graduated with a degree in science. While there, she decided to play while pursuing her degree. At Binghamton she went to take a music class but passed up the audition out of fear that she couldn't play. The teacher asked her to take the improv class and heard that she can *play* and told her she didn't need to be there, and he encouraged her to join the band: "that was a blessing because joining the band was a way for me, for the first time, to play without being judged or being criticized and treated unfairly, and I got to meet the visiting city musicians, who would ask me, what are you doing here, you have to come to New York." She met

Tia, who was playing with Beyoncé. Tia was the first woman she'd seen playing jazz. Camille's parents told her that she'd be broke if she played music, but Tia said, "I'm doing it, I'm making a living."

SOME FORMAL EDUCATION

Monte Croft attended Berklee for two and a half years before returning home to Cleveland, Ohio. He didn't have regrets that he didn't finish nor did he have any aspirations to teach. Michael Wolff said, "I was in college; I was at UCLA to study music, and they had on an OK jazz band, really nice guys . . . down in San Fernando Valley State College, which is called something else now, I can't recall. Gerald Wilson had a jazz history class." Regarding formal education, he says,

> It depends on the instrument. I think for piano, it's good
> if you have both. Also, the great people that I admire have
> both. I don't know if Thelonious Monk had formal train-
> ing, but nowadays the guys that were my idols, like Herbie
> Hancock, Chick Corea, and Keith Jarett, they're all classi-
> cally trained. I am not a classical pianist, but I studied that
> stuff, and it really helped me out as a composer to study
> music. But I think that, you know, you can't just learn that
> in college, either. I think the way jazz is now [2004], it's all
> just about education in college, which is sterile! Great musi-
> cians stand out, no matter whether they're in college or not,
> they're always going to be great. But I think, seeing that I
> got so much from hanging out with the guys, the vibe . . .

To appease his parents, Eric Reed went to college for one year. He, like Michael Wolff and Kenny Washington, weighed in most heavily on the side of learning on the bandstand:

> Not to put down the idea of formal education—I believe
> in education, under any circumstances—but I think we've
> gotten to a place where we have placed so much emphasis

on formal education from an institution that we have kind of done away with the whole middle ground of skilled workers, done away with the whole idea of apprenticeship. . . . I've heard it said, I think an attorney once told me—a guy who went to Yale University—"anything worth knowing/learning, can't be learned in a classroom." I thought that was interesting coming from him. He was not casting aspersions at education, university, or college, but making the point that information can be attained through a variety of sources and places. To place so much emphasis on a college education, you have already limited your options for learning.

Paula Kimper is a little more critical of schools:

> You can't *not* learn as you go. You have to use someone else's experience to help you teach yourself. I think everyone has to be self-taught. As far as learning institutions, I was a little disillusioned. I was put off by the whole academic approach to music, and that is why I never went to get an advanced degree. It meant writing twelve-tone music in the way they wanted you to do it; they want you to be innovative, but that is the opposite of being innovative. That's not what I want. What I hear is melodies, and I really love song forms and music that is much more accessible than what they were trying to teach. They were trying to be as inaccessible as possible. So I left that, and I've never gone back to any kind of academic thing.

WHEN FORMAL EDUCATION IS A MUST

It is rare in classical music for someone to be successful without formal education, but Dorothy Lawson has known of this happening: "That is much more difficult. I have only seen that where people got that from the family, where there is a lot of music and they got a lot of training inside the family." Every few years, I will read or hear about a virtuoso in either classical music or jazz music, so I asked Dorothy to explain what one is. "A virtuoso is a person who has control of her instrument and is so fluent and so smooth between her brain and her hands, there is no perceived block when you are listening to her playing. You are not observing a lot of work, but a lot of thought. It can be simple; it does not have to be technically showing off."

David Randolph (1914–2010), a conductor, music educator, and radio host, said,

> Formal education is very important. Nobody whom you ever heard of got there without ability. You have to have the ability! They all have their craft, in varying degrees. After that, it is being in the right place at the right time, contacts, and whom you know. I can assure you that there is competition. Like at school, like Juilliard. Everybody who gets in goes with the idea of being a big star. No one has the idea of being the second violin in the Houston Symphony Orchestra. They all want to be Itzhak Perlman. A person who studied at Juilliard told me, "It's a jungle; they are after each other; they claw over each other." How can they *not* claw at each other? When you get a bunch of virtuosos, how can they not? It's human nature.

About Juilliard, Dorothy Lawson said,

> Juilliard was a great experience. I loved parts of it. It was all-encompassing. It's a great school. They are as good as any music school, in my opinion. I was lucky that when I went, I had done so much other work, and especially that I was not an undergraduate. I noticed among the undergrads a distinct anxiety, a higher level of anxiety-driven competitiveness. They were worried that if they did not cut it and make it big at Juilliard, they would never succeed. My perspective from my travels was that they were on a

very good level, and they'd probably do nicely whether or not they were on the top of the heap in Juilliard. I didn't feel as vulnerable to that kind of pressure. The beauty of being an older student is that you appreciate your teachers more and search them out from your own interest, rather than to fill a school requirement.

NOTES

- Higher education is a choice, not always a necessity.
- Know what you want to get out of college and what kind of experience you want to have.
- At least have 40 percent formal/institution, 60 percent on-the-job training.
- Persevere, seek out mentors.
- Forge relationships with like-minded students.
- Find work outside of the school environment.
- Be committed.

CHAPTER 4

What Is a Sideperson? What Is a Leader? What Is a Producer?

Before you embark on your career, you should have outlined a plan and have a vision for your life, the kind of work you wish to do, where you want to live, and what you wish to contribute to the art form. Are you a person who doesn't enjoy working for others? Are you good at taking direction? Do you have the desire and/or stamina to be responsible for others in leading a band? Can you handle rejection? No matter your chosen field, it is imperative that you understand the requirements of the job. You have to start somewhere. At one time, the pop world was rife with sideperson-to-leader success stories; Luther Vandross, Teddy Pendergrass, and Martha Wash are examples. Luther Vandross cowrote "Fascination" with David Bowie for his album *Young Americans* (1975) and sang backup for the UK sensation in 1974. He was also a backup singer for Bette Midler, Barbra Streisand, Donna Summer, and Carly Simon. He had been singing jingles and had been the main voice of the group Change. Although the group was led by Paolo Granolio (guitar) and David Romani (bass), this was ostensibly a studio creation by producers Jacques Fred Petrus and Mauro Malavasi, who first linked to form Goody Music in 1975. With material recorded in Bologna and New York, *The Glow of Love* got the group off to a winning start, with success on the UK charts arriving with "Searching," with Luther Vandross as lead vocal. A subsequent hit for Change was "A Lover's Holiday." Following *Miracles* and *Sharing Your Love*, Luther embarked on a solo career. In 1981, Luther's debut album *Never Too Much* was released. Between 1982 and 1985, five albums were released, selling over a million copies each.

Like Luther Vandross, Teddy Pendergrass stood out. He played drums for Harold Melvin & the Blue Notes. When Melvin heard Teddy singing along with him, impressed by his vocal skills, he made him the lead singer, thus revitalizing the fledgling group that had lost popularity. In 1976, he left the group to pursue his solo career. Martha Wash may not be a household name, but you may recognize her voice on the platinum-selling hit song "Gonna Make You Sweat (Everybody Dance Now)." She achieved fame as one half of the duo Two Tons O'Fun backing up the disco singer Sylvester. From there, she and Izora Rhodes renamed themselves the Weather Girls and released the top-selling hit "It's Raining Men."

Unfortunately, the industry remains leader-driven, leaving the backup singers, well, in the dark. Morgan Neville's excellent Oscar-winning documentary *20 Feet from Stardom* (2013) follows the lives of Lisa Fischer, Merry Clayton, Judith Hill and Darlene Love, Tata Vega and Jo Lawry (whom I'd met when she sang with Allan Harris in his first iteration of "Cross That River"). Because of the success of the documentary, Lisa now has a burgeoning solo career that she is adjusting to where she has had to turn down sideperson work that she's had for years. Regarding being a backup singer, she notes, "I reject the notion that the job you excel at is somehow not enough to aspire to, that there has to be something more. I love supporting other artists." She added: "Some people will do anything to be famous. I just wanted to sing."

A SIDEPERSON

The job of a sideperson is pretty straightforward: be on time, be prepared, and follow direction. Beyond your musical abilities, your reputation (good or bad) is essential. How you present yourself will determine how much you work. You are hired "to play the music of the leader and to fulfill their vision," says Ulysses Owens. "Learn music fast, show up, be professional, do the job, and be easy to get along with." This mind-set extends to performance, as well. How you interact with other musicians onstage is equally important. I've attended my share of performances where one, if not *all*, of the musicians looked annoyed or uninterested. Believe me, that negative energy impacts the overall show. The audience sees everything! Etienne Charles suggests that "you should follow direction, unless told, don't leave the stage after you've soloed, stay engaged with the music." He quipped that the "'old cats' didn't allow a bottle of water on the stage." (An "old cat" explained to me the reason for that is because it's unprofessional. Actors don't drink onstage, it's a distraction . . .) Also, "don't be late, don't be unreliable (don't be late for rehearsal, or for a flight), and learn the music. You won't be called, again, if you don't. Don't be under the influence of any substance." The bottom line, says Jeremy Pelt, is to "know how to take direction, know how to communicate with the leader onstage, don't take the 'it's not my fault' stance, be the best ally, be on time, and dress appropriately."

Kenny Washington understands the demands of being a leader and is quite comfortable with being a sideman. He has no trouble getting work because of his professionalism and his versatile ability to work in varied musical situations. The job of leader can be a burden, and that is why Kenny has chosen not to lead his own bands. He said, "First, the way the business and the way folks are, I wouldn't have lasted because I'd have cussed everybody out. It is a big responsibility. It is a big enough responsibility to get myself and my drums to the airport on time and not have to worry about others getting there on time. I don't have patience. I don't have a problem being a sideman. As a drummer, in a big way I shape what the music is all about, though I'm not *the* leader. A band will only sound as good as the drummer will make the band sound. I have a big part in how the band sounds, and that is not my ego talking. I like being a sideman."

A LEADER

Not everyone can, or should, be a leader. An artist must be ready, willing, and able to become a leader. It takes more than sheer talent. In the jazz world, one of the biggest hindrances to becoming a leader occurs when musicians spend most of their time taking sideperson work. Being a well-known sideperson is not enough to get you to leader status. Once you've decided to be a leader, you should prepare yourself for, potentially, a temporary financial hit because you will be more selective about the work you take. In my early years as the curator for Jazz in the Garden at the Newark Museum, I had hired a prominent sideman who had made a few recordings and ostensibly had a group. Not long after our brochure was printed, he called to tell me that he had gotten a plum sideman gig that he couldn't pass up, so he canceled our date. Though I could not begrudge his decision to take the job (it paid more than I had offered, and he was to tour with a master musician), I knew that I'd not chance calling him again. "What is a leader?" Jeremy Pelt rhetorically asks. It's "all encompassing! You have to take the hits, like a quarterback in football. [You're] in charge of everything. [The leader] doesn't ask questions of the band. Having a name isn't enough. You have to be a businessperson. Hopefully, you'll have a team. And the leader has to get all the gigs."

No stranger to the demands of leadership, when Ulysses Owens decided to focus on leading a band, he took less work as a sideman but did some "low-profile" work because "people needed to see me in a certain way . . . you gotta get work, can't wait on calls like a sideman." Ulysses spent seven years working with Christian McBride in his Inside Straight group, big band, and his trio that included Christian Sands. "He really showed me what a good leader is. And he had multiple avenues to showcase himself." Taking a page out of Christian's book, Ulysses looked to curate more things. He had already started a production company set up to provide music for various settings. As a result, when the Abyssinian Baptist Church asked him to curate a vespers series for them, he was ready. He also had built a network and a "team," which is a critical component to leading.

What makes a good leader? In the first edition of this book, Ron Carter was quick to articulate those qualities:

> Number one, the example he sets for the sidemen. Is he on time? Is he dressed properly for the gig? Is he an amiable person? Two, has he learned the library of that particular band? Is he able to have some kind of input as to the structure of the tune or the arrangement? Three, what kind of personnel does he want to pick? Does he want to pick guys who are obstinate, just to see if he can break them, or is he looking for guys who want to make his music sound better? Is he willing to take less money to get the band working? Is he willing to cut his pay to hire better guys? Does he insist on only playing his music, and last of all, is he a good player?

He spent five years (1963–1968) with one of the greatest incarnations of the Miles Davis Quintet. He could have remained longer but chose to walk away.

> Well, I think bass players are generally leaders of the band, musically anyway. So that portion wasn't a difficult transition. I think that guys today [2004] who want to be leaders don't have enough sideman experience, number one. And they haven't been in a variety of sideman positions to see how different leaders handle situations. And the leaders of those bands probably aren't good leaders. So they have a disadvantage in all those areas. So I think it's difficult for those reasons. It's got nothing to do with the guy's ability or compassion to be a good leader. It's what his experience is leading to believe a leader is supposed to be able to handle.

Do you have charisma? How risk averse are you, especially financially? In 2004, Eric Reed stated that he always saw himself in the role:

I'm a leader. Since I was five years old, I was gregarious and an aggressive kid. I had an out-front personality—"Hey, look at me!" And it takes one of those qualities to be a leader. If you are a shy type, chances are that you won't be a very good leader. I was always a leader even when I was with Wynton Marsalis; in my mind, I was a leader. Essentially, even as a sideman, I was a leader—some people just have leadership qualities. Some people are sidemen; they are better at it, such as bassist Paul Chambers. Also, your instrument often dictates whether you'll be successful as a leader. Not many bands are run by bass players or drummers. They are seen as accompanist instruments. More and more, you are seeing them in lead groups, but that is still not as common. Groups lead by trumpeters and singers are more common. Art Blakey, Max Roach, Philly Joe Jones, Carl Allen, Lonnie Plaxico, Christian McBride, you have to have a certain kind of personality to be a leader. You have to have charisma, you have to connect to the audience, you have got to get to the audience in a kind of way, you have to win the audience over and make the music. With Wynton, I understood what my role was. My way to comp was interactive; I was not the average sideman who just sat back and comped behind everybody, I was very upfront. I had just as much impact as Wynton did.

Leader by Default

In jazz, the demand for singer-led groups is less popular than in pop music, where the emphasis is on singing. Vocalists find themselves in a bind. Allan Harris lamented:

Being a vocalist has its drawbacks in jazz especially, more so than in other genres. Most vocalists are not necessarily the leaders. Nine times out of ten, they are featured. The band can carry on without them, and usually does.

Sometimes they are a hindrance to what's being said onstage. The problem with some vocalists is that they feel they need to get some musicians who are adept at what they do, and that's it. They don't do their homework and bore people to death when they come onstage. That only happens in jazz. In R&B, it's a visual thing. Being a vocalist and a leader in jazz is not the same as in other genres. As a jazz singer, you are part of a team. When you are onstage, you are a part of something that is bigger than what you are.

Like Allan, who also plays guitar, Andy Bey is a pianist who began his career out front:

In the beginning, I became a vocalist, but at the same time as a pianist, but I did not consider myself a singer when I was young. But the accent became more on my vocals later on. I always accompanied myself before I joined my sisters, and we became "Andy and the Bey Sisters." They sang as a duo while I'd play piano for them. I eventually made a record by myself when I was about twelve years old. As a singer, I worked with Horace Silver for about thirty years. I did solo gigs in piano bars, played with Howard McGhee as a singer, and as a pianist with Sonny Rollins. Thad Jones/Mel Lewis, Max Roach, Bill Fischer, who produced my first LP as an adult, all hired me to work with them. I had worked one week with Max Roach, one with Ray Brown, and one with Horace at a club in Boston that George Wein owned.

Some leaders are born out of necessity. In the first edition of this book, Bobby Sanabria shared that he had no intentions to be a leader:

I wanted to be the ultimate sideman. I still am in many ways, so that is why I'm such a good leader. My job is to bring their vision across musically. The problem is that there are times when I am called to bring my knowledge of Afro-Cuban music, but sometimes people who call me to work delve into *my* world as tourists, which is disrespectful, and it's counterproductive to the music, that is, if they don't listen to me and how the music should be played. I became a leader because I could not express what I wanted to express as a musician, and I was not getting experience as a sideman. It was simultaneous, as I always did both as a drummer and a percussionist. At one point, I had to turn down sideman work as a percussionist. I am one of the best [percussionists], but I feel my voice is the drum set. Unfortunately, because my name ends in a vowel and I'm Hispanic, people tend to look at me as a percussionist, not as a legitimate jazz drummer.

I asked him if this perceptual problem made it difficult to get work. He answered, "It's getting harder because of how the record industry is. Also, when you become a leader, people don't seek you out. They think you'll charge too much or won't be interested. That is unfortunate." Since that printing, Bobby has become one of the most sought-after leaders in Latin jazz fronting his quartet and the twenty-one-piece Multiverse big band, whose recording *West Side Story Reimagined* was nominated for the 2018 "Best Latin Jazz Record" Grammy Award.

Classical Musicians

The classical world of music has different constraints in terms of musicians choosing leadership or sideperson work. Dorothy Lawson points out how she was led to become a coleader in ETHEL (formed in 1998), a group of well-established musicians in the middle of their careers who have come from different angles of the business but are all classically trained.

The violinists have lengthy backgrounds in pop and jazz and rock; the violist is an arranger and a professional from

Broadway. We love playing in string quartets, but we don't like being sidemen. We do it a lot and well, but we have a group of our own, which requires a consensus. It has been six years in the making.... I like to communicate [with the audience]. It does happen in classical where people have started their own ensembles; many quartets and groups like that are organized and held together by one person. What I am involved in now is perhaps a new spin on it, but I find it works better for people of our generation and is more of a democratic ensemble. I have preferred working in situations where I felt what I do was appreciated. That it was specifically what I do and what my personality brings to someone is why people hired me. In a way, it has kept me away from orchestral positions and situations where the premium is where one is expected to be a good soldier.

The late David Randolph surmised that by virtue of his instrument, the orchestra, he considered himself to be a leader. He was not a musician in the sense that he played the piano, or any other instrument for that matter. He explained,

Without a conductor, you would be helpless. . . . If you ask a group of individuals to sing "Yankee Doodle," they would sing different tempos, different keys. The same would be with the symphony orchestra, the New York Philharmonic, they would not know when to start, how loud to play. Music does not remain in the same tempo; it speeds up, slows down. Some instruments need to be brought out. A conductor interprets. . . . A conductor's instrument is 150 singers, a seventy- to one-hundred-piece orchestra, where everyone thinks that they can do a better job than you can; humans are your instrument. A conductor needs knowledge of the music, and the ability to get what he wants in a limited amount of time. Treat singers and players with utmost love and respect and admiration. I don't believe in yelling and screaming, the old autocratic way to be.

What David looked for in a musician was a "pleasant blending voice and [someone who] can read music at sight; sight reading is *important!*"

WHAT IS A PRODUCER?

One of the most misunderstood roles is that of a producer. I see names listed on recordings and question their expertise that warrants them the title of producer and/or executive producer. Think of the executive producer as the team leader who oversees the project from beginning to end. That person may set the budget, hire the musicians, book the studio time, hire the necessary team, and handle the contracts. The producer might direct the musical content to assist with the overall sound of your recording. Ulysses Owens has a production company and has produced various projects, including his own. He explains, "the person [producer] knows who to call, the tech person, who's gonna bring it to light, and package it. They must have lots of knowledge and know how to make things happen, not ask what needs to be done. That person creates content—is the engine."

Jeremy Pelt is "still trying to figure it out." He's been producing. He got his start doing vocalist's dates because "they didn't know how to organize and run a session, where to spend money, who would play on it, and what music they wanted to record . . . or how to work on the arrangements—all aspects of the date—including how to fix chords, the music." From there Jeremy worked with instrumentalists showing them how to best use their time. "Time is money!" Producers also keep people motivated and move things along through postproduction.

For his Blue Note recordings, Javon Jackson used Craig Street, whose music production credits include Cassandra Wilson, k.d. lang, John Legend, the Manhattan Transfer, and Norah Jones's Grammy-winning album *Come Away With Me*, of which he was coproducer. Like Betty Carter before him, Craig pushed Javon to "think outside the box." Though Javon is now self-produced, he acknowledges, "sometimes it's good to have one to hear other things." Allan Harris concurred. If he had to do his *Love Came: The Songs of Billy Strayhorn* CD all over again, he would choose a producer. "A good producer is someone who looks at what you are trying to do and thinks it through with you; two heads are better than one. You do what is best for that project. I can get hung up on certain kinds of things of what I think is right. In hindsight, I would have put something in another place or done it another way. I might not have done that had I had a good producer who would help me do that, see it another way. I have had good producers in the past who have done that."

THE MUSICIAN AS SELF-PRODUCER

With today's technology and major labels folding, musicians have taken more control of their artistry by going it alone and/or starting their own record labels. They have also taken advantage of the Internet as a vehicle for getting their product out. In 1988, when Monte Croft was signed to Columbia Records, the label acted as producer. He was new to the label and fought to produce his albums because he didn't have confidence in their ability to package him properly. The role of a producer, he explained, "is the organizer but it varies from recording to recording. He/she can choose the players, suggest the players, choose the material, or can suggest the repertoire or stay out of it. The person books the studio, where to place the instruments, the mics, etc., the programming of music after it's recorded . . . some are more hands on than others." Monte had come to the attention of George Butler, who was one of the most important A&R (artist and repertoire) men in jazz. Wynton Marsalis had been signed to Columbia. Monte had played a gig with him, on vibes, at the Village Vanguard that George had seen. Armed with his demo, he met with George, who signed him on the spot.

They didn't have a vibes player on the label at that time. The deal dropped in my lap. I wanted to produce the record, there was pushback on that, though. Then I was the youngest artist to produce myself, on a major label, in jazz. None of the other guys produced their own records. I was learning on the job. I had to use their engineer and their studio . . . I knew what I wanted to do. I had just produced my own demo. . . . It came out all right. For my first production, I think it want really well; by the second record, I'd gotten better.

NOTES

- Understand the role of a sideperson, a leader, and a producer.
- Choose a producer who understands your concept and how to execute it.
- As a leader you are responsible for everything!
- As a sideperson your job is to show up, be prepared, and be easy to get along with.

PART TWO

ON COMPOSING, ARRANGING, AND RECORDING

The secret of writing a good popular song is to make it
melodically simple and harmonically attractive.
—Jule Styne

CHAPTER 5

The Art of Composition

The *Encyclopedia Britannica*'s definition of composition is "the act of conceiving a piece of music, the art of conceiving music, or the finished product. These meanings are interdependent and presume a tradition in which musical words exist as repeatable entities. In this sense, composition is necessarily distinct from improvisation." The process of composition is a personal one; to some it comes easily and quickly, for others it may take time. Music of the Great American Songbook, which tells the story of the first fifty years of American popular music, remains prominent today. The songbook contains some of the best of George Gershwin, Irving Berlin, Lorenz Hart, Richard Rodgers, Oscar Hammerstein II, Cole Porter, Harold Arlen, and many more artists. Other great modern songwriters not included in the Great American Songbook lexicon include John Lennon and Paul McCartney, Stevie Wonder; jazz masters such as Thelonious Monk, Benny Golson, and Duke Ellington are often sampled, while classical composers are celebrated and revered. Johann Sebastian Bach is one of the greatest composers in Western music whom I listened to as a child and still enjoy. His music "swings."

What makes a good or even a great song? How are songs written? What are the mechanics? The terms "composer" and "songwriter" are sometimes used interchangeably. Ron Carter suggests that the elements essential in writing a song are "melody, changes, and form." Pianist Cedar Walton is considered to be a wonderful composer. He wrote such standards as "Bolivia," "Mode for Joe," and "Fantasy in D"—also known as "Ugetsu." Regarding Cedar's music, Kenny Washington told me that "what makes Walton's songs so good is that they are difficult for a musician, but easy for the listener." Ron Carter's response to that comment was "No, Cedar writes a nice melody, and he has good arrangements of those melodies. That's what's so attractive." He continues, "I think everyone knows they can write. Whether they want to develop that talent by taking lessons is another story." Ron developed his writing skills by "taking composition lessons, arranging lessons, absolutely!" Also, he is not above asking for feedback from those whom he respects: "I don't mind going to Benny Golson and saying, 'Benny, is this arrangement OK? How's this work, or why doesn't it work?' You have three or four guys in New York who I would call up and say, 'Can you help me with this?' The problem is that most jazz players don't take composition lessons; they think they don't need them, and their compositions aren't any good."

Pianist Kenny Barron is another well-known writer whose songs have been covered by many artists, but he is quite humble when discussing his work.

> I don't think of myself as a composer; I'm still working on it. I'm trying to write for larger ensembles. I'd like to do more of that . . . I'm happy when others record my songs, such as "Sunshower" and "Voyage." What makes them work is that they are basically very simple. When you look at hit songs, not that mine are hits, the songs are very simple melodic lines. I don't see myself as a composer; I write tunes.

On his approach to writing, he remarked, "I can't force the process. Sometimes all of the elements will come at once, and sometimes I get a germ, and I follow it in a direction. I can't just sit and write a song."

A challenge of a classical composer is time. Dorothy Lawson says:

> I write when I have something that's coming up that I
> have to write for. I write on a computer, and I'm pretty
> fast. I tend to write a form that is bracketed by true com-
> posed stuff but has improvisation in the middle, so I'm
> not writing everything out. Improvisation [in classical]
> music is coming back now. In the Baroque period, the
> great composers—Bach, Handel, and others—were huge
> talents as improvisors. Most of their music was made up
> as they needed it. For example, the great violinist Corelli,
> a famous traveling virtuoso, once published his famous
> pieces. They were skeletons, sketches. It has been an
> anomaly, in classical music, over the last hundred years,
> where people have tried, through sophisticated means, to
> subvert the natural sense of rhythm.

For Paula Kimper, writing "was a process; I heard music. So I knew I could do it. When I was a kid, my biggest fear was that I would write something down that someone else had written because I heard it. Part of my reason for going to Eastman School of Music was to learn what was out there so I would not copy." When asked about her writing new music in opera, she said, "It's a dance, like in jazz. The downside of attempting something new in opera is the expectation of the audience. They say they want to hear something avant-garde, but then if it's too avant-garde, they don't consider it opera. If the music is too standard, then it's not avant-garde enough. My first opera was referred to as a folk opera."

Composer Mikael Karlsson pointed out the distinction between orchestration and composing. "Orchestration, I get help with that, it's the hardest thing, my composition teacher said, 'that's the thing you'll never be done learning about.' We study it (maybe two semesters), but you have to learn that on the job. It's something I don't know enough about that I should hire someone. I've used the same orchestrator for five years now. I think you have to either play in an orchestra or con-duct an orchestra to be a good orchestrator."

On composing, he explained,

> I don't think there's an art to it in the spiritual sense, to me
> it's a craft. If inspiration hits—great, you have to learn to
> write without it. I don't think it's that ethereal, my process
> is pretty logical. It always starts with improvisation, it's
> fluid. After that is application of knowledge. The focus is
> to be conveying something interesting enough for people
> to keep listening, it becomes about rhetoric. We did an
> opera where the second act was a stream of consciousness.
> Tobias Packer said we should meet his librettist to help
> us [younger people] with it. He pointed out that our idea
> wouldn't work, as it would have been one woman sitting
> in a chair, screaming, for forty minutes. My task is not
> to lose their [audience] attention. I never compose from
> theory, I'm a dramatic composer, I tell stories whether
> abstract or not. I think of an experience, I improvise. I
> end up with a lot of shitty ideas and find a few that work.
> Now, with my skill set, how do I make this work? How
> do I keep spinning the same thread so I don't try to be
> more complicated then I need to be and don't be plain
> enough to bore people? How do I make it interesting to
> *me*? But that's secondary. I rely on the listener thinking it's
> worthwhile (where I check my ego, I know what's it like to
> take the time to go out when I could have been watching
> Netflix). I learned from Alex, he wants people to have a
> good time. That's gotten lost along the way in classical, it's
> way down on the list. It's surfacing again, people realize
> we're in show business. No matter how we want to pack-
> age it, we're entertainers.

MUSIC INSIDE—IN THE ZONE

Others also acknowledge a spiritual dimension to writing—when
their best work comes—as being "in the zone." Ray Charles said in

his 1978 autobiography, *Brother Ray*: "I was born with music inside me. That's the only explanation I know of. Music was one of my parts, like my blood. It was a force already with me when I arrived on the scene. It was a necessity for me, like food or water." Early in his career, Jeff Clayton learned what is called "the empty vessel theory" from the late jazz drummer Billy Higgins and also from Stevie Wonder. He explains,

> There is a place where we can go, like a big empty vial, or a vessel, that has everything creatively that we want in it floating around. Our job, standing outside the vessel, is to make ourselves open and aware, and to educate ourselves on how to read the ideas, or the notes and rhythms that are in the vessel. When we go there, if we can identify them, we are allowed to pick them out of the air as they fly around and place them in a medium that will allow us to write them in our head or on a piece of paper and play them for others. It means that we don't own what we create; we simply, out of the universe, identify those elements that were here before we got here and will be here long after we are gone. The proof of this concept, for me, is that I write songs that are far above my musical understanding, because I made myself as aware as I could and taught myself as many things as I could about music, so when I get inside this vessel I can identify them. Some people never even make it to the vessel. It is a coveted place where music is created for those who are open and aware enough to accept the music that is being created.

For those not musically trained, he explained,

> There are notes, rhythms. . . . There are two parts in writing: one, the craft, how chords fit together, where they go, the augmented, the "demented" or rather, diminished, the mechanical information. Two, there is pure inspiration,

which is mixed in with those notes that are floating in that vessel. The wind from the vessel is the inspiration. When you put your hands out, what sticks to your hands are the things you understand enough from being outside the vessel, learning about the music that allows you to put them together into a song. When you pull them out of the vessel, they are still in raw form; it is your ability to write and rewrite—that is the craft part. The information and inspiration is in the vessel. The things with chords that you thought would never use, or the notes you thought would never go together, work perfectly. If you know nothing about music, and you go in and see a bunch of notes, it is gibberish. The empty vessel is divine inspiration with divine information, only accessible to those who are open and aware. You dream a dream of beauty and grace, and when you feel that warm breeze across your face, then you sing—you are in the vessel. The singing that comes out of your mouth, you work hard to let your mind remember and write it all down.

I have witnessed musicians who can sit down and write songs on command and asked Jeff about that process. For example, John Hicks wrote "After the Morning" in forty minutes on his way home from the famed jazz club Bradley's. Erroll Garner was on a plane to San Francisco, California, when the melody for "Misty" came to him (he couldn't write music, so he had to hum it to someone who wrote). Upon reflection, Jeff replied,

It depends on where you write it from. Some write from knowledge only. Once you become aware that it exists, you can access it; it is difficult at first, but the more you do it, the easier it is to access it. As soon as you figure out how it feels to be creative, you can go anywhere and access the force. You will find that it comes when you are not thinking; it is a mindless awareness. When I was with

Stevie Wonder, when the creativity came over him, it was so big that it would include the rest of the room and stop people from talking, and we did not know why we had stopped. That's deep.

Richard Smallwood draws from an emotion when he composes songs: "Some of my most difficult times have birthed songs. Writing music that speaks to people comes from a deep well of emotions, experiences, faith, hurt, disappointment. Those songs probably touch more people; you write from that place, it's spiritual. The essence comes from a deep place coming from your knowledge of music. It connects to the person who hears it. I get more feedback from those songs than any other songs." He is not particularly methodical when he writes: "Sometimes I just get a melody in my head, usually I'm nowhere near a piano. I'm in a hotel, in my car—the melody will come when I'm shopping, so I have a device on my phone where I just record and develop the melody when I get home. At times, I'll hear a phrase, secular or from a sermon, that will spark the creativity in me. It comes in all different kinds of ways."

Always interested in writing/composing, Etienne Charles was taught in college. Beginning in his sophomore year, his teacher, Rodney Jordan, had the students writing songs—from a blues to a thirty-two-bar tune, up-tempo tunes, and ballads—and they would perform them. (This taught him about how a leader picks a set; John Clayton, Marcus Roberts, Monty Alexander, and Marcus Miller are great at putting together sets.) Etienne did an independent study with Marcus Roberts, who helped him develop his concept of "expanding," where lots of his musical roots came from the Caribbean. His concepts are "about making a statement as a composer to honor the tradition I grew up with." Roberts had him write a suite based on a theme that Etienne included in his first album, *Culture Shock*.

Writing Lyrics

Writing words to music is its own skill; not all musicians can or do write lyrics. For those who do, I ask, what comes first, the words or the melody? I posed this question to Jeff Clayton; his response:

"When the melody and the harmony and the lyric come at the same time, it is a gift from God. That means that the song will be spiritual. It just comes to you—where did it come from? If it comes from intellect, then just try to do it again. If you can't get back to it, it was not you at all. Otherwise, if one thing comes first, it is usually the melody before the lyric."

Inspiration comes from different places. In 2002, Allan Harris began work on his epic musical, *Cross That River*, about a runaway slave named Blue. He incorporated several musical styles that were relevant to the time period in which the story was based: the blues, jazz, and country. His writing process was thus: "The idea came first, then the lyrics came second, then I put the melodies around the lyric. I played it first on the guitar; I heard bass, guitar, and violin. As I got to know the songs better, the other instruments came later. I listened to Lead Belly, T-Bone Walker, Charley Pride, Allman Brothers; they influenced me a lot." For his 1995 release, *It's A Wonderful World*, Allan had cowritten a song with bassist Ray Brown, who insisted that Allan include one blues on the recording. Under pressure, the night before the recording, the song "Black Coffee Blues" came as he sat drinking a cup of coffee. He recounted,

> I had one night to do it; it happened over a cup of espresso, it just came to me, like "Mule Skinner" and "One More Notch." I don't know where that comes from; that happens a lot when you have a creative flow. Usually those songs are the best—they come from a place inhabited in your mind. You are not writing to please an audience, not to fit a bill; it just happens to be in your psyche.
>
> Look at "Oh Happy Day" (Edwin Hawkins). It was a blockbuster hit and only had three basic sections: the verse, the chorus, and the tag, and just one chord/four chord. The nation was just ready to embrace it. It is crossover gospel. If you have to put it in a category—first, it had a choir, in the gospel vein, but it had Latin, jazz, pop, soul overtones. Just because it has overtones does not

make it that. If you take water and put lemon in it, it does not make it lemonade, but it is water with lemon flavor. That was the trend of the day, so "Oh Happy Day" marked the beginnings of what came to be called contemporary gospel. Before that were the gospel quartets such as the Dixie Hummingbirds, Clara Ward Singers, and Mahalia Jackson; it was such a much more narrowly defined sound. André Crouch, Reverend Hawkins, Rance Allen were in their midtwenties—young people—and they began to use their influences like Sly and the Family Stone, The Beatles, Rolling Stones, so just by default those influences seep in.

NOTES

- Study composition.
- Have the listener in mind.
- There is no formula to writing.
- Have a concept.
- Allow inspiration to kick in.

CHAPTER 6

The Art of Arrangement

A specific performer or original interpretation can make a song memorable; that process is not completely dependent upon the writer's talents. When Ray Charles passed away in June 2004, several performances were held to honor him and his music. Jeff Clayton played on two of the events and commented, "Ray Charles *knew* how to pick good songs." Though he was not known for his writing, he could turn almost any song into a classic. Ray Charles was an innovative singer and pianist who combined blues and gospel in a way that pioneered soul music and earned him the nickname given to him by Frank Sinatra, "the Genius." A partial list of his hits includes "Hit the Road, Jack," "I Can't Stop Loving You," "Busted," "Makin' Whoopee," "I Got a Woman," "Drown in My Own Tears," "This Little Girl of Mine" (covered by the Everly Brothers), and "Let's Get Stoned," the first hit for the singer/songwriter team Ashford and Simpson. His version of Hoagy Carmichael's "Georgia on My Mind" was named the Georgia state song in 1979. One of the most moving recording was his rendition of "America the Beautiful."

Ruth Brown could also pick good songs. Often she sang songs brought to her by fellow musicians. "Frank Wess would say, 'This is a good song for you,' the musicians would come out with the arrangement, and we'd swing." She and Ray Charles were good friends, and he advised her wisely, "I won't tell nobody, but *I like you very much* because you are singing what people know, and you are singing, and people know what you are singing about!"

Eric Reed observed in the first edition of this book that

> Jazz musicians have recorded those songs of Sting, the Beatles, Stevie Wonder, and such. A great song is a great song, and it depends on how it speaks to you. A musician did an arrangement of "One," a Marvin Hamlisch song. I'm not a big fan of Hamlisch's music, nor was I blown away with the guy's arrangement of the song. There's nothing that says that you can't take that kind of a song, and if you have any intuition or creativity, you can make it into a masterpiece. Who knew that Ramsey Lewis would make a great hit out of "Wade in the Water," an old Negro spiritual? He turned it into this crossover hit. It does not matter how complex or simple the song is.

One such song, covered through the years, by the songwriting team Jay Livingstone and Ray Evans, is "Que Sera, Sera (Whatever Will Be, Will Be)." It was introduced in the 1956 Alfred Hitchcock film, *The Man Who Knew Too Much,* sung by Doris Day. It was a simple song that won the Academy Award for Best Original Song and became Day's signature song, which she used for her sitcom (1968–1972), *The Doris Day Show.* In 1973, on their *Fresh* album, Sly and the Family Stone recorded their rendition, giving it a funky, soulful sound. The song has found a new, modern, urban iteration on bassist Marcus Miller's Grammy-nominated release *Laid Black* (2018), which combines his signature sound with elements of present-day music drawing on the Black musical experience. I must admit that I like *all* three renditions. All resonate with me. The first two evoke memories of my youth; Marcus Miller's version brings me into the present.

Arranging is the adaptation of an existing composition for performance on an instrument, voice, or a combination. Jazz is replete with prominent big band arrangers: Sammy Nestico and Neal Hefti for the Count Basie band, Billy Strayhorn with Duke Ellington, Benny Carter with Fletcher Henderson, and others. When Bobby Sanabria taught Manhattan School of Music's Afro-Cuban Jazz Orchestra, he focused on arranging. Out of that class came his award-winning adaptation of the masterpiece *West Side Story*. He recalled,

> In terms of *West Side Story Reimagined*, the germ of it came about twelve years ago, when I did a concert at Manhattan School of Music with the ACJO, based on movie themes. It was called "Latin jazz in the movies." The concert was constructed around melodies from different movies done in various Latin styles. The last song had to be the mambo scene from *West Side Story* as a cha-cha-cha. So I assigned the arrangement to my student, baritone sax player Danny Rivera (he was a budding arranger at that time who had showed a talent for it while in Fiorello H. LaGuardia High School of Music & Art and Performing Arts). I told him what I wanted him to do, and he did it. The gym scene is composed of many aspects. One is the opening scene, where you see the gangs dancing to a slow blues in a big band style like the Count Basie Orchestra. When [the character] Tony walked into the gym, both bands were dancing (I told Danny to include the blues), then it morphed into the mambo. Before it goes into the mambo, there's a kind social worker named Mr. Gladhand played by John Astin (of hit TV show *The Addams Family* fame, and I think this was his first film role) trying to bring both gangs together. He had them in a circle facing each other, so when the music stopped, they were to dance with the facing person. [The attempt at unity quickly faded away; it didn't work.] The next scene was the music/dance exploding into the mambo— the most exciting scene in the movie and the only time you see both gangs in ecstasy . . . the reason why is that

the music brought everyone together. Like in the 1950s (*West Side Story* debuted September 26, 1957), it united all cultures. For me, the thing was to capture the intensity of the Basie band, then exploding into the mambo but orchestrated and arranged for my big band and then to feature the musicians as a soloists. We tell the story without any lyrics. There's very little singing (except on "Maria" and chanting on "Jet Song"). The whole story was told through the rhythms, not the lyrics. My intent was to update the score, which was a hard thing to do, because Leonard Bernstein's music is so advanced; hard to do. It's the most difficult score written for a Broadway show, as it combines lyrics, opera, chamber music, and vaudeville with jazz and Latin music and was done in a cohesive and authentic way. On top of that, *West Side Story* is really a ballet created by Jerome Robbins.

To put a fine point on arranging, Michael Wolff keeps it real simple. "Be cautious. Do not use the same chords."

NOTES

- Don't use the same chords.
- Be creative.
- Take chances.
- Add your voice to the piece.

CHAPTER 7

The Purpose of Recording

Is the CD dead or on life support? Vinyl is making a comeback, as are brick-and-mortar stores. They are not only surviving the digital age, but finding growth. Statistics from retaildive.com suggest that we cannot discount the fluidity of consumer purchasing choices or their need for a physical product, be it a disc or an album. On April 13, 2019, the retail industry held its twelfth Record Store Day, on which stores across the country hold music events and special releases. Retail Dive elaborates on the background of the annual celebration:

> After nearly fifty years in business, record store chain Tower Records shuttered in 2006, and the number of independent record stores dwindled to some 2,000 in the U.S. But in the past five years their numbers have grown again to about 2,400, Wes Lowe, an executive at wholesale CD, DVD and vinyl record distributor Alliance Entertainment Corp., told the AP.
>
> Many of the stores are in smaller towns, and much of the business is driven by a resurgence of vinyl record sales, according to the report. Vinyl album sales have risen from annual sales of fewer than one million in 2005 to more

than 13 million last year, according to Nielsen Music research cited by the AP.

The endurance of independent record stores is akin to the survival of independent bookstores, which have similarly survived two decades of disruption from Amazon. Their numbers, too, have increased in recent years; both bookstores and record stores have found ways to compete by hosting local events at stores and positioning store staff as helpful experts. Bookstores and record stores also benefit from the surprisingly successful and enduring "buy local" movement.[1]

Recordings have less impact on your career than in past decades. At one time (up until the mid-2000s), an artist's life centered on getting signed to a major label and touring. Unfortunately, labels were notorious for ripping off musicians and binding them to long-term multiple record deals. Stories of musicians, unknowingly or naively, giving away their rights were commonplace. It took a young and enthusiastic Richard Smallwood many years before getting a record deal. However, he was hoodwinked into thinking that he'd landed a great deal with Blue Note records while a student at Howard University (though it is not a laughing matter, he had me in stitches as he told me the story): "When I was in college at Howard University in Washington, DC, I was part of the first gospel group on the Howard campus called the Celestials. Donny Hathaway was one of the organ and keyboard players and singers, and when he left, I stepped into his place. It was all about making demos. We made a demo. Since we knew no one in the industry, we took a Greyhound bus to New York City, rented a room in a YMCA for ten dollars, got a phone book, looked up all of the record companies within walking distance, and knocked on doors. We were a bunch of college kids." One interesting thing happened on that trip to New York City. "We got to meet George Butler, who was at Blue Note, and we got to play our demo for him. He listened to what

---

1   Daphne Howland, "Brick-and-mortar record stores stage revival," *Retail Dive*, April 21, 2017, https://www.retaildive.com/news/brick-and-mortar-record-stores-stage-revival/440989/.

I had, and he told me that that I was ten years ahead of my time. He said, 'What you are doing, no one else is doing.' He told me, 'Keep doing what you are doing, and you're gonna make it, I *promise* you.'"

The story continues. After meeting with George Butler:

[We] ended up at the record company that had recorded the Chi-Lites, and we were let in. A man listened to our demo, took us around the company, and said that he would sign us. There were no other people in the office at that time; he claimed that they had all left for the day, but he promised that he would send us the contract in three weeks. We left to go back to school, and our friends gave us a record release party—balloons and all. My manager followed up and was told that there had been a flood, but that the man would get around to it. After a series of delays, the contract never came. A year or so had passed, and one of the acts from that label came to DC. We went to the show and talked to the performer and told him our story. At first he did not know who we were talking about, but after our description of the man, he roared with laughter and said that the man was the janitor! It was devastating back then, but funny now. It's all part of paying dues, but you have to keep plugging away. . . . It was almost ten years to the day after my meeting with George Butler before I got my record deal. I kept making demos but never heard from people. One year I did a concert in Kentucky. The promoter later went to work with the Benson label (a Christian label) and called to see what we were up to. The label was looking for black artists to sign. The president had us come to Nashville to lay down tracks on the studio. We drove down on a Thursday, and on Monday, we handed him a tape, and he signed us on the spot. We knew nothing of attorneys, so we signed.

WHEN TO RECORD

A recording always has value. It is a document of your work and an example of where you are musically at a given point. Before you record, you must ask yourself what Derrick Lucas of Jazz 90.1 references as the journalistic questions: "who?" "what?" and "why?" Who is your audience (or desired audience), what do want to play, to record, and why now? Assess your growth. Artists may record too early in their careers, artistically speaking. It's a personal choice. After years of sideman work, Michael Wolff made his first recording at age forty. Established artists such as Allan Harris find it necessary. He exclaimed,

> Of course! That is the life's blood, the fuel that keeps this machine running. I have three just this year on the table. I am always trying to find the time to write and then choose the musicians who will gel together for a certain sound I am hearing. That takes time, so I might cherry-pick who is going to do a certain tour with me based on what I need to hear for the next recording. It's a lot of fun when we find our niche with a tune and know we are on to something vibrant and exciting. Once every tune that I am doing live meets those criteria, that's when I feel it's time to record some magic!

WBGO music director and announcer Gary Walker, who previews all music sent to the station, feels strongly that one should record "when you are truly comfortable inside your skin, not from what people tell you are comfortable with your craft. And you must be inspired by your own craft . . . not because of a parental rush to get them out there." Note to you parents who control your teenage children: *Do not load up their first CD with special guests!* Let your child shine based on their talent, alone, not on the force of special guest stars. That creates a train wreck and can result in minimal airplay because the "CD will sound superficial as if you're spending too much time on success and not craft . . ." Gary Walker saw Stevie Wonder when Stevie was twelve—after he recorded "Fingertips." "He was amazing. They put him on the bandstand. . . . It wasn't about attention or success."

Be true to yourself! Aaron Diehl encourages artists to have a "sense of integrity, musically and financially. Record contracts are done. People are putting out their own stuff. Justin Collier became an Internet sensation, first. . . . It's good to document yourself. Cecile McLorin-Salvant [with whom Diehl collaborated with for years] just puts stuff out there so people can see and hear her development." Musicians must become more recording-savvy. You have to understand what, when, and why you are going to record.

While he was a college student, Mikael (Mika) Karlsson decided that he would showcase his work simply by sending clips of it to friends. That was a wise move on his part because people shared it with others. You never know where it will lead. For Mika, it was to a fantastic job opportunity. "My path was to start making things before I graduated. I became interested in documenting things very early on and packaging them. It showed my body of work. I had a few recordings of a few pieces. I made a website and kept sending my CDs to all of my friends. . . . A friend who was doing video games liked my music and asked if I had a team . . . 'I'm in charge of music for a video game, one of the biggest games at Electronic Arts, the game called *Battlefield*; I like your music, do you have a team?'" What transpired from that inquiry was a game changer for Mika. You can read more about this in Chapter 15.

In hindsight, Eric Reed wasn't ready when he produced his first CD in November 1991. His reason was simply because Alan Bates of Candid Records asked him to. At that time, Eric was shy, and he felt that it was too early in his career to have made that trio recording because he "didn't have a repertoire." By the time he made *It's Alright to Swing*, he had developed a conception of arranging. When he recorded *The Swing and I*, he'd found his voice . . . "Jazz, like gospel, was born of a culture and an environment. Music is a way to express emotions. Once it became a commodity and put on a disk to sell, it became a product, the essence and intent was lost forever. Now it's become art. When no longer functional, it's useless. The music suffers because of the way it's presented [Eric is considering that he will perform live and never record again.] Mingus preferred live recordings." At this stage in his life, Eric Reed wants to break free of the confines of the industry. He's also happy that he continues to get royalty checks from some of his records. By 2011 Eric was burned out. His recording *A Light in Darkness* came from so much that had been happening in his life at that time. Being a beacon of hope, joy, and peace globally. He always wants to be cool and push through the negative.

Remember, there is no right or wrong time to record, and the length of time it takes for you to record is arbitrary. It took Camille Thurman three or four years before she recorded her first CD, *Spirit Child*, in 2011. It was released in 2013 on Hot Tones Music (distributed by Mimi Jones's label), CD Baby, and iTunes. No stranger to the business, Camille understood that she didn't need to make a CD and that a press kit had become antiquated, but she was starting to tour and needed something to sell to her growing fan base. "Now there's more streaming; no money in that. You have to fight for what you're owed. [The good thing about] radio is it lets people know who you are and that you exist." A savvy promoter and excellent businessman, Etienne Charles believes "You have to have a reason to record. . . . I will make a video when I record to show online so people can connect to a story and they connect better when watching." He records because he's a composer, and it helps him get new gigs. "Radio will play you more when you have a new record out. I used to record every two years then every year. Don't record just because." Etienne recently released his seventh release, *Creole Soul*, and it garnered high praise. "In the wise words of Michael Wolff, 'Record as much as you can.' [However] Anyone *can* make a record—'The mediocre are always at their best,' said Jonathan Winters. You gotta compose, write your own music, and record."

Be realistic; though recording is not income generating, Dorothy Lawson, cofounder of the classical group ETHEL, considers it necessary. "Recording is vital, for advertising, marketing and sharing your product, but it does not make money. ETHEL publishes a new album about once every three years. Single cuts and videos are more useful."

WHAT TO RECORD

Determine why you want to record before you go in the studio. Do you want something to sell at gigs? Or to have for promoters? Do you have airplay in mind? If so, consider the following: the length of songs; the repertoire. Will you record all new music? A mix of standards and new? Whatever you decide, you should have your audience in mind. What experience do you want them to have? Gary Walker, music director and weekday morning host on WBGO, Jazz 88.3FM, shared his thoughts: "As it pertains to jazz music, if you are a new artist, do not make a recording of all original tunes; people need familiarity." Prior to talking to Gary, in 2004, I had asked Eric Reed to respond to Gary's outlook on emerging artists' recording standards. He said, "I wish, if this is the attitude of announcers—that new artists should play standards—that they get rid of it. It just puts limitations on the music, which should have no limitations. Wayne Shorter and Horace Silver both have well-documented recording of standards. Horace's first CD has standards, and Wayne's first was originals, but he did one standard. He recorded 'Mack the Knife,' 'All or Nothing at All.' Down the line, they began to establish recordings of original material." Gary's viewpoint, in 2019, has slightly changed: "[The artist] should still include a standard—don't box yourself in, could be a Sting tune or Stevie Wonder or the Beatles—a contemporary artist." The reason why contemporary smooth jazz is popular is that, for the most part, that music is vocal tunes played instrumentally, which resonates with many people.

To you jazzers, "Swing is *not* passé, it's not dead, it still works, and brings the listener in." So says Derrick Lucas, program director, announcer, and account executive (given the full-time staff of four, he wears many hats) at Jazz 90.1. A big fan of Arthur Taylor's insightful interview book (one of *my* favorites), *Notes and Tones*, like Taylor, Derrick poses the question, "What comes first—you, the musicians, or the audience? What's your priority? Their answer will give me an idea where they're coming from . . . it has to move me emotionally. Do I *feel* something? Are they covering things like Great American Songbook? Or the Black American Songbook if they're doing Motown, Stax? I'll preview those CDs with that music first, it's *our* music. If all original tunes, it has to *swing*. I look for Pitch, peace, power, if it makes me feel good. If I'm in a car, will I listen or turn the station?"

"The more things change, the more they stay the same." In the first edition of this book in 2005, Ron Carter talked about audience tastes and their appetite for "concept" records. Conventional wisdom advises against them (I haven't found empirical data to substantiate that sentiment). What was true in 2005 remains true in 2019. He said, "Your CD has to tell a story. Yeah, I have a story, and I record the songs in the order of my story. For me, that's I how I do it. Other guys have different views and approaches. I've gone there with a story to tell; when the last song is done, my story is complete, and I only hope that the company will agree to that order of songs on the final product. . . . I noticed the absence of liner notes on CDs, something that many old-timers like me miss most. Sitting and reading album jackets was a joy and a learning experience." I asked Ron why they have almost disappeared, and he replied, "I miss them. It's cheaper not to have them. You don't pay for a writer, and it takes less paper for the inside information. I miss those days of information listed with musicians' thoughts about the songs and their tunes and the information that's necessary to make the listener feel he was part of the session."

Some artists draw from life events for inspiration. All of Tia Fuller's recordings are a reflection of benchmarks along her path. Her first Grammy nomination for *Diamond Life* was born of having survived some years of turmoil and emerging a better human being. "All of my releases reflect what is happening in my life. . . . Recordings document where you are, and are a product to show, it's a time line of your life . . . my first recording, *Pillar of Strength*, came a few years after I'd moved to New York City." Likewise, Eric Reed, a sensitive, brilliant, reflective, and thoughtful human being, uses his art for healing.

Classical Music and Radio

Whereas in jazz and contemporary radio, new artists can find a home on terrestrial radio, not as much on classical. The percentage of classic tunes versus new music on WBGO is 75/25, on Jazz 90.1,

70/30. WQXR is the largest classical station in the country, and its hard-core audience wants to hear the standard repertoire. Weekday evening host Terrence McKnight discussed audience demands; "They like standards. Each year we survey the audience for our 105 year-end countdown where they pick their favorite pieces. You get music that starts around 1800–1930, *maybe* 1950, *maybe* an Aaron Copland piece in there. Let's say 150–175 years of music is what classical music lovers cherish the most. Beethoven—top ten, Brahms, Tchaikovsky, some opera composers like Puccini and Verdi [are in the mix]." On the topic of new artists breaking into classical (their mix is 90/10), "I know artists on the scene in their twenties and thirties, like Yang Ying or Jennifer Higdon, they're playing the standard repertoire. They [audience] don't mind a new artist as long as they're up to speed and just as good as the old standard. . . . Audience demographics are fifty-five and older, 55 percent women, 45 percent men, 75 percent white." In order to attract newer and perhaps younger listeners, WQXR added a new digital music stream, New Sounds, dedicated to all contemporary artists. Dorothy Lawson doesn't minimize radio's significance as it pertains to her: "Radio airplay is important, as is any medium where an audience will spend time experiencing and appreciating your work. It must be measured for its social value."

CDs VERSUS DOWNLOADS

Musicians are struggling to adjust to the changing landscape of a shrinking CD demand. For various understandable reasons, some have chosen to abandon burning them, instead opting to create "download only" releases. Today's technology makes it easier for musicians to produce their own product, but CDs are still desired, at least for radio consumption. Michael Wolff understands this all too well. His most recent release, *Swirl* (Sunnyside Label), came about from a live performance at Yamaha Studios, an event hosted by WBGO. He acknowledged that "the recording process hasn't changed. . . . If you want to be on the radio you still need a CD." A movement is afoot where artists are recording downloads only. I applaud musicians like

Linda May Oh Han, who are choosing that method for environmental reasons, but it would help if they burn a few recordings for radio use. (You can read more about the importance of presenting your music in the right format in Chapters 14 and 17.)

Again, Gary Walker contends that musicians should consider burning some CDs for radio stations: "Avoid downloads—wait to send hard copy, technically speaking, although it's only in the preview setting. We still rely on 30K compact discs. . . . Don't let anyone tell you that the CD is dead. . . . It's still the optimal way to get your CD out, but how many people will really receive it? You're representing your music with an iTunes mentality," meaning fewer and fewer musicians are providing liner notes, thus not telling the listener their story. What's your story? From the perspective of the presenter, it helps when you tell them something about your music and yourself. Think about the end user. Radio people are bombarded with product, so how will you stand out? Give them a reason to listen to your recording. At the risk of sounding old, I have fond memories from my youth of sitting on the floor by the console, listening to music and reading the backs of albums. Other reasons to record is that it may help you get gigs and provide a documentation of where you are musically.

CD Cover Design

Content matters! For me, a radio announcer, CD cover design is a pet peeve. I implore you to think about the end user before you design a CD. We are overrun with product that we can't read! Please, do not let the design interfere with the text. Too much emphasis is placed on the color scheme, photos, drawings, and other fancy design elements at the expense of text legibility, rendering the information useless. The user should not need a magnifying glass to read the credits and/or liner notes. Heck, I have written several liner notes that end up on CDs that I can't read. It is staggering that, I'd say, 75 percent of the CDs we receive can't be read because the type is too tiny, and the color (or lack thereof) is neon and runs together. The information is so crammed, we practically have to take notes from the liner notes. If it can't be read, it may not get played. Don't make us conduct research to present *your* product. (More on radio in Chapter 14.) Also, if you choose to package it without text on the spine, it may get lost on the shelf. WBGO has over one hundred new releases in our studio; if there is no spine, it's easy to get lost in the shuffle. Again, think of the end user.

Consider the following:

1. Do not use yellow, red, or purple type over a black background.
2. Avoid a serif typeface, especially if it is white dropping out of a dark background.
3. On the back panel, write the number for each song. Add the correct time of each.
4. Write the *full* name of the writer. For example—Oscar Brown, not O. Brown.
5. Include liner notes, even if short. We want to know your story and something about your recording.
6. List special guests on each tune. We want to be able to announce them. Avoid writing a numbered laundry list of musicians. For example: "Musician A on bass (tracks 1, 5, 8, 9); Musician B on all tunes (except 2 and 6)." We don't have long to back-announce; it is inconvenient for us to have to search through a laundry list for the information. Instead, how about this:

   Track 1: "I can't get no" (3:54)
   Written by Full Name. Full Name on vocals; Full Name on bass; Full Name on piano; and so forth.
7. The record label should be easy to read: Such and Such Productions, XYZ Records, etc.

NOTES

- Before you record, have something to say!
- Your recordings should have a focus.
- Record a familiar tune—anyone from Sting to the Beatles to Stevie Wonder.
- Familiarize yourself with your local radio stations and the announcers.
- Find out who's playing your music around the country (hire a radio person to track airplay).

PART THREE
ON PERSONAL GROWTH

If you have patience and knowledge, and if you are aware of all that
is happening around you, you will gain something unexpected.
—Alhaji Ibrahim Abdulai

CHAPTER 8

Self-Assessment

No man has a chance to enjoy permanent success until he begins to look in the mirror for the real cause of all his mistakes.
—Napoleon Hill

What *is* self-assessment and why is it important to one's growth? In order to move forward in anything, in life, we must look inward to determine what to discard and what to develop. Digging deep is not easy, but it is necessary. If you are not getting desired results, the earlier you reflect, the better. Be honest about your positive and negative attributes, who you surround yourself with, if you need more training. . . . I was a precocious child and seemingly scattered and unfocused about my life. My mom cautioned me to "sit down and take stock of yourself." A man of many talents who lived to be eighty-four, Benjamin Franklin demonstrated honesty and integrity throughout his life. It is he who allegedly coined the phrase "Honesty is the best policy." Perhaps his reference was to people to be honest with others, but the most honest relationship should be with ourselves. Apply that personally to be *honest with yourself* about everything, including your talents and the most effective way to use them. Conversely, it is incumbent on those whose advice is sought to be truthful with those who seek information. Yet too often, those who claim that they want to hear the truth are really looking for validation. Richard Smallwood shared a story about a woman who wasn't open to his assessment of her. Having been sensitive to others' cruel comments (when people sought help), he tried to be fair with one woman in particular:

> People come to me all of the time with demos. Some time ago, a singer with bad pitch gave me her demo, but she could not carry a tune in a bucket. She had a problem with her intonation, so I suggested that she get some voice lessons and ear training. She came back to me and said she had done what I had told her to do, but she was worse than before. (Can't people hear themselves?) She told me that people said that she was no good, but until *I said* that she was no good, she would not listen to them. I told her that she was not up to par; she got mad and did not speak to me again, but I had to be honest.

From birth to death, we travel a jagged road, not a straight line. "Life is full of little triumphs. People don't stand in line to hear the truth! People will pay for BS (the truth hurts)," Eric Reed lamented. Set benchmarks along your way. Stop, then evaluate. Jeremy Pelt was clear: "Self-assessment is necessary! Be honest with yourself, especially when you hit a plateau. How to get to the next level? What do you need to do to improve and get better? Have a goal for what you want to get out of your career. Always have something new to work on. Pinpoint your weaknesses if you need to. Or turn your weakness into a strength. Have to go forward with positivity. Be honest that it might not happen." You will know when you are "there." At thirty-six, Ulysses Owens has always been introspective; he continues to do the work toward personal and musical improvement. "Be honest with yourself. Self-assessment is being real. Have a hunger and desire to be better. Know when you're ready for things, to go to the next level. Be open to others' opinions of you. Talk to others who've done what you want to do. Be open to advice." Also, Dorothy Lawson considers the opinions of her peers to have importance. "Oh, yeah. For me, my long search was to take all of those opinions to try to understand what the relationship between their responses and my own perceptions was, and to get a consistent idea of where their point of view might be coming from."

When life's challenges take their toll, step back and remember your goals. Tia Fuller set goals very early in her career. Every few years, she would revisit her plan and affirm if she was reaching her marks. In 2005 she, like Camille Thurman, had gone into a deep depression. The events that led up to her funk helped her "let go" and realize that she had to control it. Years later, she hit another low. She'd begun teaching at Berklee College (2015). Both her booking agent and manager dropped her. Tia needed a break. Work had slowed down and she was working less, so they let her go. "I had to rebuild a team and that's why it took me six years in between recordings. (Both parents were sick, and I was going back and forth)." *In the Trenches* came out of that experience.

Motivation is also a source to draw from when faced with adversity. A spiritual and contemplative man, Andy Bey uses that as his driving force:

> How you become motivated, and how you lose motivation, is a choice. You can make excuses and judgments; they are understandable, but if it affects you, it is about you. There are a lot of disappointments and a lot of pain. It's the purpose, me making music, what I was put here for. It can't just be about music; it's about the person dealing with the music. You must take care of all aspects of your life. I must take care of my health, my spirit, my consciousness. If I don't, then I'm not supporting the music because I'm not taking care of myself.

REDIRECT/SHIFT GEARS

Learn to know thyself. Learn to own up and accept your limitations and find a way to create within those boundaries. Disappointments can turn into triumphs. What appears to be your biggest challenge may be your most valuable strength. Be careful how you process information to avoid becoming a victim. Are you one to determine that others are to blame for your circumstances? Do you often tell yourself that "others just don't get me"? Are you one to spend more time looking outward than inward? The reality is: all of these scenarios can be true at the same time, *but* if you are the only constant in your stories, you may want to point your finger back to you. At a point in my life, I felt that I was going in circles. Frustrated, I talked to my friend Harvey Wise, who simply said, "Sheila, if everyone says that you have a tail, you should turn around." Those words resonated with me. They were the push I needed to on my path of self-discovery.

At the height of Living Colour's success, they were selling sixty thousand units a week. Thanks to the Rolling Stones's giving Living Colour the opportunity to open for them, the industry came knocking. Sony signed them, and they recouped their money early, so they continued to invest in the band. For the most part, Will felt that they'd been honest brokers, though he confessed that when they didn't want to sell CDs in South Africa (because of apartheid), three times they caught Sony moving that clause (that they *would* sell in South Africa) to another part of the contract. For eight years, Living Colour had a great run. Their third record was a huge success, so when Vernon Reid abruptly broke up the band, it was a shock to everyone, including the label. Will says,

> It was a difficult time for me, I was still young. I left the States for a year and went to Australia to be around [Aboriginal artist] Michael Nelson Tjakamarra because I was attracted to him and his art. I stayed out in the bush, stayed with about eight different families. What was great about that time away was it gave me a chance to look at myself. It was also the beginning of me looking into any future relationship that I'd get into, I learned that I needed my own space, my own private Idaho. It was five or six years of me being down and bitter, brooding.

When Eric Reed found himself at a crossroad, he was shaken. His dream was to be a world-class, working, jazz pianist making records and touring the world and to work with his heroes. One January night, in 2006, he went home after a gig and began staring at a wall in his apartment. "The sun was coming up and I was still staring at the wall. I hadn't slept. It was unnerving." Eric had attended a concert, not a gig, where he could hear a voice—"move out of New York." He was not enjoying himself, was reserved, stiff, and the musicians didn't look like they were having a good time. The audience wasn't enjoying itself either, and it left, too. For two years he'd been thinking about moving. He knew he couldn't stay in New York City and had a two-year ordeal of deciding. Eric didn't want to leave his friends or his stature in jazz. But he was unhappy. He realized that "I had neglected my humanity and ignored my maturity and my own growth; it was stunted."

MUSICAL GROWTH

Adversity is cleansing. It gives us perspective. Before turning to opera, Paula Kimper traveled many musical paths:

> Opera is really the last genre that I entered. Everything is a kind of process. . . . I got a bachelor's degree in trumpet performance; I was a trumpet player. The trumpet was loud, and I could be in the band. It was kind of ego-based in a way. I moved to New York [City] in 1979 and went into pop music. I played piano, used a custom synthesizer, had my own studio; I could do it all myself. That led me into film scoring and doing music for theater. I liked opera, listened to opera broadcasts, and I was in opera in college. When they needed stage bands, I played in the orchestra.

After a great success in Miami, Istanbul, and other places, Allan Harris tried his hand in New York City but had little success. He dug deep to understand what went wrong.

I was not well received, not by the audience. I did not know how to present myself, what to say onstage. I was too abstract; I was not directed and focused. New York was not into fanfare like Miami. It took me a few years to shed that, and the residue is still out there. I was making a good living out there [in Miami]. I saw myself drifting into the sunset. It was a challenge, and I got my butt kicked. I brought that small-town mentality to New York, thinking that that was enough. I got the starch taken out of me. I realized that I had homework to do, and I had to grow as an artist.

I reached out to Allan to follow up. I said, "You had shared your story about that evening at the then-popular club Tatou, where Tony Bennett was in attendance. You bombed, driving you to do some serious soul-searching." He replied,

I now call it keeping my chops tuned. I am never going to be the next Jimi Hendrix, Pat Martino, or the great Chet Atkins! There was a time in my youth that I fantasized and flirted with the dream of maybe one day being mentioned in the same breath as them. The more I came in contact and exchanged musical experiences with my peers, I began to realize I had a hard decision to make. The first was to put down the guitar for a while to more fully understand and concentrate on my growing vocal prowess. Writing "Cross That River" on acoustic guitar was cathartic for me and reminded me how much I missed playing. So I've been incorporating more guitar into my performances, and it makes me very happy. Oh and yes, keep the Tony Bennett thing!

Quality versus Quantity

I began my work life as a production assistant. After two years, I was promoted. Having only worked at Random House for four years, I got the job of manager of production at Grove Press, where I had a horrible nine-month run. My next production job at John Wiley & Sons was equally painful. A job at W. H. Freeman opened up as I was reaching my one-year mark at JWS, and I was thrilled. There was a problem . . . my résumé reflected six years of production experience, but, in fact, I had two years' experience, three times, so I was woefully inexperienced for that job. Had it not been for my patient supervisor, Ellen Cash, I may have gotten fired, especially after an oversight of mine cost the company $4,000. I had to be honest with myself; I did not like production work! But my ego would not allow me to be the weak link of the department. After some soul-searching and hard work, I learned how to do the job and immensely improved in a relatively short period of time.

What does this have to do with being a musician? I have encountered many who have worked for years, some twenty plus, who have not grown musically and/or professionally. They tell me, "I've been doing this for X number of years, I've worked with so-and-so, and so on and so forth." They bellyache about the work they are *not* getting rather than being grateful for the work they *do* get. ("Funny," Art Blakey told Javon Jackson, "If you're working, you're doing something right.") What they lack is an ability to self-reflect and self-assess that leads to their victimhood. I say about victims that they're all alike. They have a tendency to accuse others of actively working to impede their success by awarding gigs to others that they believe they deserve, or they believe that people are jealous of them. Here's the rub: sometimes the work you don't get has nothing to do with you.

In reality, according to Eric Reed:

> Self-assessment is not simple. What I've come to discover is that there isn't a whole lot of work for the number of musicians there are. And folks are dying. What I've found is that there are phenomenal musicians that *do not* work; it has nothing to do with ability. Sometimes it's an inability to connect to influential people or to connect to people who are working, or an inability to network. Often the

powers that be have an agenda so the way the industry works they're figuring out how to make money. If it don't make money it don't make sense. They'll put their money behind an idea, behind a movement, but rarely will they fund an artist who has something musical to say. They'll fund a look, fund an image, they'll support that; not the music. In the 1980s it was the image that sold jazz. They had to call it something, so they called us "young lions." The thing is that, regarding self-assessment, you have to be around musicians who will be honest with you. Part of the problem in the jazz world is that ability is subjective. In European music, either you can play or not. Nobody mediocre will wind up onstage being featured with the L.A. Philharmonic playing Brandenburg Concertos. If you sing at the Met, you have your stuff together. In jazz you can *be* mediocre. It depends on the musicians. If you're playing with musicians whose focus is bebop, for example, yet you come with an approach from Albert Ayler or Eric Dolphy, they'll throw you off the stage. Young musicians should be held to a standard to play the music. The things that Ron Carter requires in his bands [aren't necessarily] what Chick Corea requires in his: jazz is subjective. Billie Holiday had no range, but she sang her truth; I listen to her to hear emotion. The best singer is Sarah Vaughan—there *is no such* thing as the best singer in jazz. Miles Davis kept you guessing. He said Blossom Dearie was the only white woman who sang with soul—*what*? Rosemary Clooney, Anita O'Day . . . ? So many people treated Miles like a god. What came out of his mouth was gospel, what he put out was curriculum as far as so many people were concerned.

Speaking in a general sense about music, Eric made a case for an industry cleansing, of sorts, among musical genres. "They still study the classics (Bach, Beethoven) but Duke Ellington, not so much. Janis Joplin screamed and spit her way into a career," he chuckles. Also,

"Robert Glasper and Kamasi Washington are making people aware of *their* music. A good thing. No one artist should take the burden of an entire field. Every artist must be true to himself, be honest, be genuine, have integrity, and give people something of substance." You just have to learn to accept what is (I know that isn't easy) and keep working on your craft. To quote my friend, comedian Wali Collins, "Y'Nevano!"

NOTES

- *Be honest* with yourself!
- Do some soul-searching.
- Talk to people whom you trust.
- Learn.

CHAPTER 9
Ego Check

Ego is a person's sense of self-esteem or self-importance. It is defined as the view that a person has of him- or herself. It takes work to be even-keeled. I am no exception, as I constantly work to keep my ego in check. Years ago, Javon Jackson turned me on to the book *The Four Agreements* by Don Miguel Ruiz, and it has proved invaluable. I had to read it a few times before I was able to remember all four of them. Based on ancient Toltec wisdom, the book offers a powerful code of conduct that allowed me to be more relaxed. They are: *Don't be judgmental, Don't take things personally, Be impeccable with your word,* and *Always do your best.* I must admit, the most challenging for me are the first two. How do you see yourself? Are you one of the greatest musicians on Earth? The greatest performer? Working in the field of entertainment, when I encounter folks consumed with their own self-importance whose talents don't match their bravado, I hear the words of vocalist Ernie Andrews: "You aren't who you think you are." A healthy ego is good, but an unhealthy ego can foster toxic behavior that will turn people off. It is easy to become consumed with one's own idea of greatness, significance, or importance.

Etienne Charles and Jeremy Pelt have a similar view on this topic. Jeremy observed that

Wynton Marsalis is *now* cool, but in the eighties and nineties he was (considered kind of) a jerk. You gotta get past it. You must have some ego. Trumpet players are groomed to be leaders because of the nature of their instrument. We don't always get called. We can't be the nicest guys in the world. The industry isn't nurturing, after a point. We need bullies to make us better. Ego is a protection against other people. Have to know when it works and doesn't. Trumpet players have been called arrogant. You have to believe in yourself before any others. It becomes more mental. He has to sell himself. Talent is the deciding factor, but you have to sell it.

"Ego is the first line of defense and first thing to give you confidence gives you the tool to say, 'F it,'" said Etienne Charles. "When it becomes toxic it affects how people see you in a negative light. I've always been around people who kicked my ass [he claims that his musicians are better at their instruments then he is at his]. Professors keep kicking my butt and why my ego is in check. Then I'll listen to 'Pops' (Louis Armstrong) or Lee Morgan and being around elders and keep quiet, they give lessons. We are a tribe who makes this music. All of us in the music are in the tribe." To keep grounded, Ulysses also looks to those who came before him: "It keeps my ego in check when I see the greats, living artists like drummer Roy Haynes. I look to what my attributes are. . . . I am confident in who I am and the kind of artist I am. I always want to be better, I admire the masters, I never arrive. Ego has been the death of great musicians. [Know] that the industry is fickle."

Tia Fuller spent six years (2006–2012) in the band of pop diva icon Beyoncé, and she had to work hard to keep her head on straight as she observed the negative impact it had on other band members. One member, in particular

was doing the best she could, but I'm not sure what happened between then and now. To play at Zinc, she asked folks to get her a limo, she was "Beyoncé-fied." Getting a gig like that, if you're not stable or grounded, it can throw you off psychologically because you can become that and think, 'cause what you're around you become that thing. You're wrong, you're a bystander of your situation. Being with Bey, you get all the perks, but it's not because of your workmanship but with the artist and can get it twisted. I went through it for a moment. I was comfortable, though I was still booking gigs, had that steady paycheck coming in and but wasn't able to let go that I had to keep my legs steeped in the jazz world because I knew that the Bey gig would end someday. I admitted that this is a stepping-stone, not a destination point for me. Some people got it twisted.

Camille Thurman has accomplished so much in a short amount of time. For years, female musicians have led movements against Wynton Marsalis and Jazz at Lincoln Center (JALC), accusing them of discrimination for not hiring women except as special guests. Camille landed the job (she's filling in for someone for a year). She worried about how others would react to her getting that job: "I thought that they'd be mad at me, and I worried about how I'd be accepted. In the end I had to 'bring it' and do a great job."

TALENT VERSUS POPULARITY

"*I have an inflated ego,*" says Aaron Diehl with a laugh. "Hearing others pushes me to get back to the drawing board. Younger musicians don't have older musicians checking them and what they do. There's less mentorship now." As a child, I was told to not get a big head—talk about self-esteem and being told that you are good! Being popular doesn't make you good. To you musicians in your teens, be careful of what we would call "too much, too soon." If you stop growing artistically, rest assured, when you get into your twenties, someone younger will be taking your place. You may attract a large audience, have hit a record or two, and get great press. It *will* end should you stop learning. Case in point: This is an excerpt from the first edition about a young man whom I'd met, who was then barely out of his teens. I had just begun my job at the Newark Museum. He had a good reputation for being nice, polite, and respectful. That young man approached me, seeking to play at a venue where I produce a jazz festival each year. Several people had told me that I should talk to him because he was really good and that I needed to listen to him. He was very sincere and explained to me that he was just beginning to seek work as a leader, and that he would send me something. What he sent was quite shocking. His package included two demo CDs, a photo, and a letter that did not contain anything close to proper standard letterform, or even Standard English. The typeface was a fancy serif typeface, and he ended several sentences with a smiley-face symbol (to my shock, another artist sent me a letter with the same symbol at the end of some sentences—whew!). As I said, he was asking me to consider him for a jazz gig, but he included some samples of hip-hop that he had done, and his jazz sample was him playing to Jamey Aebersold music. That alone showed that he was not close to being a professional. It would have behooved him to have rented a studio with his friends and taped a live session. And he needed to consult someone on how to write a standard letter that was grammatically correct, as well. If you do not know what to do, then ask someone who knows. Years have passed, and he is an adult. He is still playing but hasn't really advanced musically and is frustrated that he's not working as he thinks he deserves. Because he's unable to reckon with his lack of skills, he's decided that his lack of work is due to his race.

HUMILITY/BE HUMBLE

Being an artist is perhaps one of the most fragile professions in life. So much of what artists do depends on how accepted they are. Artists have died penniless, only to have their great work discovered after their death. Not all artists seek validation through public acceptance. Thelonious Monk said, "I say, play it your own way. Don't play what the public wants. . . . You play what you want, and let the public pick up on what you are doing, even if it does take them fifteen, twenty years." Aaron Diehl said, "You have to have humility, that is nothing new! Share with love . . . have a sense of integrity."

To that point, some advice from Ron Carter to young musicians:

I tell the students this story. I did a recording session where the musician was not very interesting or very good at promoting his musical ideas. I proceeded to play in a fashion I felt made the music sound better and made the arrangement give more life to the song. But then the arranger came in and said, "I like the way you played, but I want you to play what I wrote." So I did. I tell my students, "No matter who you are, if someone hires you, you better be ready to do what they tell you to do." The moral of the story is, no matter how big you are, if the guy writing the paychecks tells you that you play shitty, you just have to live with that. I had a sax player in my class who played just average, and I would get on his case all the time, and he was not doing what I asked him to do. He got a job as a reviewer for a magazine, and he bombed my own records. That's personal, but it was in print, and no one knew the background of the writer reviewing my record. Those things come along, for me, to keep my ego in check and not get blown out of the water.

Eric Reed talked about turning down an opportunity to work with Ray Brown (after leaving Wynton):

I had made it all about myself, didn't think I had the right to turn down Ray. I manned up and said no. That's when I moved into being a leader. . . . Ego check? It isn't about me, there have been great musicians playing this music. . . . I have to always remind myself that what I'm doing is trying to express beauty and love to people. Can't let your ego get in the way. Love and ego can't occupy the same place. Can't give to people when you're always trying to get something. People shouldn't be guarded when you're onstage. Gotta work through stuff. There's healthy ego that makes you keep going.

Dorothy Lawson keeps herself grounded by understanding why she is a performer: "I guess it does all come down to the question of what I'm trying to do as a musician. I am not there just to have people look at me onstage. I'm there to share emotions with people—that excites me. If I did not have the confidence to think that I could do something, then I don't know why I'd be there."

Richard Smallwood does not feel that his music comes from his ego. Rather, he feels that he is a privileged vessel for the inspiration, Word, and music of God: "I never have dealt with that ego, but I know that it exists. It is a privilege to do what I do—why I was picked? I don't know. It is a sacred trust God has given me. My ministry extends off the stage; it can happen in the grocery store. You have to be where people can reach you. You get tired, don't want to be bothered, I just stay home." He told the story about one of his first workshops at the Smithsonian Institution, which was quite humbling for him: "The crowd was mixed, and when it ended, a white lady who had been sitting in the audience told her neighbor sitting next to her that she had contemplated suicide that morning, but after hearing the music, it changed her life, and she realized that her life was not her own. She was inspired to learn more about God." This happened early in his career and colored how he felt about his ministry. He says, regarding working with other musicians, "I can't be all things to all people, but I can be nice to them. I love my peers; I admire all of my peers. There is room for all of us, and what they do does not diminish what I have. There are people I've worked with who had big egos. I let them know that they were no better or worse than anyone else, but they were blessed because they had the good fortune to be chosen."

DON'T BE A HARDHEAD

Allan Harris confronts his ego constantly. He admits, "I'm still working on it." In Chapter 8, he referenced a show that he'd done at a club called Tatou in New York City, where Tony Bennett was in the audience, that turned out to be a huge ego buster for Allan:

> Sammy Cahn introduced me, and *it was terrible!* It was the most embarrassing moment I've ever had onstage. I fought Tony Bennett later that night. He had wanted me to take lessons and take my show to Luther Henderson. Luther and his wife, Billie, were in the audience on the invitation of Tony, who had put the evening together, and they wanted me to come over to their place and work on my show, and I had an attitude—*imagine that!* It was real deep. I had not yet moved to New York City, but later, when I did, we [Luther, Billie, and Allan's wife, Pat] broke bread again, and Billie told me that night was terrible; I was all over the place. After that show, I went back to Miami; I had a few years to marinate; my phone did not ring. I had to go back to the drawing board and shed a lot. Ego is a hell of an impetus, because when you see someone really good, there is a balance between their ego and their talent. You want them to have an ego and to be confident in what they are trying to say. If they are self-involved and not worried about entertaining, they are almost masturbating, and the audience is a voyeur. Pop singers can't do that because they are concerned with the visual show. But exceptional jazz singers can really let the audience watch them practice their craft. For the other 70 percent of artists, ego gets you to the stage, but if your craft and talent are not in sync with your ego, you have to drop it *when* you get to the stage so you can connect with the audience. The audience helps you out and brings you out of it.

Update: "[Now] I embrace it! Muhammad Ali said, 'Braggin' is when a person says something and can't do it.' I do what I say. I do what I say. Enough said."

BE GRACIOUS AND GENEROUS

Mika says, "Don't put all of your eggs in one basket. Can't afford to be angry with people who say no. It's OK to fight for something, but folks don't like to work with angry people. Business is more transparent, play clean. Always say thank you, don't be too humble, don't talk people out of the good stuff you do." Growing up, how many times was I told that it's easier to attract bees with honey than it is with vinegar? Adults made it clear that to be pleasant went a long way in life. Attitude and approach to *all* situations were drummed into me and my friends. Specifically as it relates to the jazz community (this applies to life), I have seen musicians blow opportunities because they appeared aloof or rude to people; some were, some were actually shy. Ask for feedback on how you are perceived. You may need to make some behavior adjustments. However, no matter how much tweaking you do, in the end, don't take things personally; it is not always about you.

NOTES

- Be grateful, show gratitude.
- Learn to forgive and let go.
- Let go of your need for control.
- Be self-aware, not self-centered.

CHAPTER 10
Success and Failure: Have Perspective

The people who make it to the top—whether they're musicians,
or great chefs, or corporate honchos—are addicted to their
calling . . . [they] are the ones who'd be doing whatever
it is they love, even if they weren't being paid.
—Quincy Jones

Do you consider yourself to be successful? What does success mean to
you? What is failure? Can you have one without the other? The difference between success and failure is patience and persistence. They set
goals, make short- and long-term plans, monitor their progress, and
revise as needed. If you aren't getting desired results, don't give up.
After reading an article in *Jazz Times* or *DownBeat* magazine written
by the late pianist Geri Allen about the term "a crystallized vision,"
Tia Fuller learned that goal setting was what she needed to do. At
Spelman, freshman year, she decided to move to New York City.
Before embarking on that journey, she took a detour and enrolled at
the University of Colorado in Boulder for a master's degree. There
she met Byron Stripling, who was giving a clinic. He had the students
close their eyes, dream of the venues where they wanted to play, how
it smelled, etc. The second exercise he had them write where they

saw themselves in ten years; visualize, then write their ten-year goals. They had to be specific. Ten years later, Tia reviewed her list to find that she had hit almost 98 percent of those things. She didn't anticipate working with Beyoncé but had a clear direction toward the level of musicianship and about the people she wanted to be around. "I tell my students at Berklee, 'Through your vision and determination you will be blessed with abundance, just do the work.'"

One cannot overestimate the importance of hard work. Mika Karlsson heeded the advice of a visiting professor emeritus at Queens College, where Mika was a student. He said, "I'm going to leave you with some wise words from the New York philosopher, Woody Allen: 'The most important thing in life is for you to show up.' And that has so many levels, not just in life. [It's] being there and letting people know what you dream of, your aspirations. Things happened, partially because of luck, but to grab it you have to be prepared (luck is when preparation meets opportunity)." Without question, disappointments and rejection are inevitable, but how you respond to them is key to your success. Mistakes are essential; you must learn how to *not* avoid them in order to extract the information needed to continue on your path.

You may ask yourself, *why* am I *not* successful? Even if you don't ask yourself this question directly, you might experience moments where you compare your achievements to those of other people and become dissatisfied. One of the most important factors that can help a person become successful is learning how to tolerate failure and move on.

Unbeknown to me, my father was hoping that I would learn to fail at a young age. At age sixteen, I was asked to run for the New York State youth president of the NAACP. I had only been the Buffalo chapter president for two months and had just entered my junior year in high school. Uncertain that I should run, I called him for advice. His words to me were: "Sheila, if they want you to run, you should run." To my and *his* surprise, I won. After my first term, I ran again and won. He and I talked about my reelection, at which point he said, "Sheila, the only reason why I told you to run is because I thought

that you'd experience defeat at a young age, but you keep winning."
Needless to say, I found his revelation shocking and revealing in that,
at that point, I couldn't process why losing was a good thing. Years
later, I understood. At age nineteen I was elected Region II youth
member to the national board of directors of the NAACP, where I
served two years. When I was not reelected, I got depressed; it was
the first election that I'd lost. I had allowed my identity to be defined
by titles, not by my soul.

Loss and failure are emotional. In the first edition of this book,
Allan Harris addressed the pain:

> Failure is hardest to move beyond. Rejection is *not* good
> for the soul—it's B.S. Failure is a truth serum. You never
> get over failure; you harness it and use it as a reminder of
> what you have to do to move beyond to become success-
> ful. You forget successes, so people remind you of your
> successes, especially when you are in a slump. Failure is
> compounded when you have another failure. For some
> reason, the baggage of all other failures come with each
> new one. Artists think that all failures are related, but
> they are not linked; each has its own seed. Failure is won-
> derful; it's debilitating, but, yes, you can get past it. You
> can wallow in your lack of success, or the drive to be suc-
> cessful can be so great that you are able to smother that
> feeling of rejection. Rejection causes us to feel numb. It
> paralyzes a lot of people and keeps them from making
> that next call.

For this edition, I was curious to know if he still viewed failure in
the same way. His response:

> I will say my opinion on failing has not changed, just
> the way I might describe certain hurdles I've crossed
> and some that have tripped me up. To use the old adage,
> "pick yourself up and dust yourself off" is the mantra I

have been living by since I realized failure, at least for me, has been a most valuable tool. Yes, I am calling it a tool, for I use failure to reshape and help build the lesson plan that I will use in my next foray into the creative battle for success. Believe me, I am constantly waging it. I know this is kind of long-winded of me, but there you go! I embrace failure, it is and always has been my most valuable teacher.

To that point, Jeff Clayton remarked, "I don't consider failure. I consider everything information. Each time you gain information, you educate yourself. There is no failure."

Two of the most successful artists today, Beyoncé and Lady Gaga, have some insight on failure:[1]

> In the words of Beyoncé: "The reality is, sometimes you lose. And you're never too good to lose, you're never too big to lose, you're never too smart to lose, it happens. And it happens when it needs to happen. And you have to embrace those things." [. . .]

> When it's not as easy to embrace those setbacks, though, you can remember this anecdote Lady Gaga told about getting dropped from a record label: "I remember when I got dropped from my first record label. I just said, 'Mommy, let's go see Grandma,'" Gaga told MTV in 2011. "And I cried on my grandmother's couch. She looked at me, and she goes, 'I'm going to let you cry for the rest of the day, and then you have to stop crying, and you have to go kick some ass.'"

---

1 Marissa Muller and Jane Burnett, "Failure Is Part of Success, Especially for Women," *Thrive Global*, February 26, 2019, https://thriveglobal.com/stories/women-failure-success-fail-forward-advice-resilience/.

WHAT IS SUCCESS VERSUS BEING SUCCESSFUL?

Some dictionary definitions:

> Success (noun)—favorable or desired outcome[2]

> Successful (adjective)—gaining or having gained success[3]

There is no exact answer to this question because it is personal. You determine what success is to *you*. Is it financial? Is it popularity? Is it career success? To have good health (mental and physical)? What was your reason to become a musician? Aretha Franklin told my friend Joe Madison, the "Black Eagle" who hosts the eponymous talk show on SiriusXM, "In order to be successful one needs to be three things; be original, be authentic, and be courageous." Though Javon Jackson doesn't necessarily agree that one must be "original," given the number of musicians who we know are successful without that trait, he believes that one should "be humble, consistent, and willing to do whatever you do and do it all day long. . . . [At the end of the day] you will be able to look yourself in the eye."

The three attributes Jeff Clayton believe makes a successful musician/artist are ability, business acumen, and drive. If you don't know where you're headed, how can you measure success? Like Tia Fuller, Eric Reed suggests that you need to have a direction:

> I say you have to define what it is your goals are, your vision, your mission, how do you plan to do it. What are you doing *currently* to get to your vison? If you want to be a world-renowned superstar celebrity, good luck with that. The vision is the measure of success and should be more realistic. . . . There are various defining factors of

---

2   *Merriam-Webster*, s.v. "success," accessed August 28, 2019, https://www.merriam-webster .com/dictionary/success.

3. *Merriam-Webster*, s.v. "successful," accessed August 28, 2019, https://www.merriam-webster .com/dictionary/successful.

success—developing, honing, and shaping the skills to continue the mission to achieve the vision. My dad was a successful husband and father. We had a home, we were fed, clothed, clean, and we were loved. There is no formula!

In regard to the genre, Eric continues, "The pop world doesn't teach you how to focus on yourself. You are a viewed as a commodity. Nor is it a requirement for you to be proficient on your instrument. Emphasis is placed on your image." According to Eric, "the problem with the music industry, in general, is that it *is* an industry, which denotes commerce. Often the powers that be have an agenda, so the way the industry works they're figuring out how to make money."

The pressure of success at an early age can be daunting. Edwin Hawkins, to some degree, felt its weight. In his twenties, his rendition of "Oh Happy Day" became what was considered an overnight sensation, by taking gospel music to the secular world. He said, "There are pressures. I remember very well. Like Buddha Records trying to take another song and make it into something with the magnitude of 'Oh Happy Day.' You cannot re-create that. I believe that God did it alone. We recorded it on a two-track machine in a church; what was the likelihood of that happening again? People understood the component of a successful record, but to re-create that is a greater challenge."

A MATTER OF PERSPECTIVE

"Neither success or failure are permanent," says Eric Reed in the first edition of this book. "They can be lasting or very brief. Some people keep coming back. People's careers take dips, and trends change, the economy changes. You can look at this in terms of changing seasons. Success or failure is too extreme, too definitive. Stevie Wonder and Duke Ellington will always be respected as musical geniuses in everyone's mind. Just because they stopped producing great things doesn't mean they stopped being great. Some people don't know when to stop; they don't know when they've worn out their welcome and need to go reinvent themselves and go on to something else."

Paula Kimper questioned my asking her about overcoming success: "A trick question—what do you mean? That's personal growth. You don't have the right to expect that anything good will happen. If good things happen, then you treat it as a gift; you can't think that you should get a gift every day. With opera, it takes so long. I have to put anticipation on hold while I do my work, and it takes years. I don't feel like I'm not getting anything. I don't think I've gone out of style. It's part of it to be out of it for a while then come back."

"Do you believe in failure?" I asked. She replied, "It's definition—I don't talk of failure or success. A lot of good things have happened along the way. I feel I've been confirmed in my path by the universe. I kind of had that experience after my first opera at the Lincoln Center Festival in 1998. It was a really big success. It sold out, people got standing ovations, and there was a lot of press about it. I went home in August, and nobody called me for months and months, and I thought, Isn't something supposed to happen next? It was like the feeling of, nobody is looking now. So I realized I had to make another piece, and I had to call people."

LIFE CHANGES/CHALLENGES ON SUCCESS

Relationships

Ulysses Owens thought that he needed to be married to be successful. He thought it would

give me stability. When my marriage was wrecked, it wrecked me, and I lost almost everything and the little bit that I had. And I completely survived. . . . Divorce taught me to be incredibly uncompromising, and I took it as a blessing. Not having a marriage allowed me to be incredibly selfish and to only do the things I wanted to do and do it when I wanted to do it and build the things I wanted to do. I completely threw myself into things. If I'd been married, I don't know if I'd been able to have a business, in New York City and in Florida. My ex-wife is an actress, and she also had a freelance life. It's hard as an artist when we're both out here juggling and having to both take risks. I met someone who was, like, "You want to be great, I want to be great too," and it became a tug-of-war.

I see where it works in other artists' marriages (like Allan and Pat Harris). Young musicians need to be careful about relationships. I see some mentees who have amazing young women who are in love with them, they are "ride or die," who hustle with them, they're holding it down. I'm doing better now and am hard pressed to share and ask, "What are you bringing to the table?" Musicians need to understand that you only have a certain amount of time to focus. When you're young, make sure that your energy isn't all over the place. If you find someone who understands and loves you through it, that's great. But if someone is taking away your focus or your energy when you should be in the shed or be thinking about strategy, or how to be better, I see people lose that. Some would rather be in love than have a career. That's OK, too.

Be careful who you let into your life. There are countless musicians who have been sidelined by personal issues such as marriage, divorce, kids, etc., which forces them to have to take unsatisfying work and/ or have to work tirelessly because they need money. Mika Karlsson observed his collaborator become bitter when he "got a crazy wife and had a kid," forcing him to take work he didn't enjoy and that took him away from composing. Eric, too, realized the upside of divorce: "Now I turn down most jazz things because they're not things I want to do. I'm busy doing other things. But I can turn down things because that decision only affects me, and I sleep like a baby at night. I don't have to prostitute myself because I need the money." When faced with adversity, Ulysses turns inward: "What helps me get through adversity is I'm a person of faith, not religious (I used to be). That's what keeps me going and instills character. . . . I see life as seasons. Life has ups and downs, that taught me lots, and I learn from my mistakes."

Illness

German philosopher Friedrich Nietzsche wrote in *Twilight of the Idols*, "That what does not kill us makes us stronger." Michael Wolff knows that all too well. In 2011, he was diagnosed with a grueling and bewildering form of cancer that on the outset had left him bedridden for eight months. Blessed with incredible insurance from the Screen Actors Guild (his wife, Polly Draper, is an actress) after one year of being sick, he finally went to Sloan Kettering, where he found a doctor who saved his life, as he'd had been previously misdiagnosed. The subsequent years toward recovery were hell, but his will to live was strong. I remember when I called Michael in March 2015 to hire him for the Somerville Jazz Festival in September. He hesitated to accept the offer because he had been ill. I hired him anyway, believing that he would recover by then. "That was my first gig after being sick," said Michael. "I was so happy to be back on the stage, all my friends were there. . . . It was a long journey. I felt *so* happy onstage at Somerville, I felt fantastic when we did that gig, it saved my life, I got through it."

Cancer free since 2018, he considers himself "one of the lucky ones." His outlook on life and his priorities have shifted.

> I'm sixty-six. From all I went through, I have a different view of things and am so appreciative of all the people who have been so important to me. . . . I got to play with great people and I still love it. Each day I notice something special. My doctor said, "enjoy every second." . . . Illness gave me a will to live. I was always a realistic optimist but didn't know I had character. I had never been in a life-or-death situation. Being in bed eight months with no end in sight, no cure in sight. To get through that, I say, "You are tough!"

Contrast his perspective on success and failure in the first edition. He said, "It's a mixture. My life is so successful, I'm so lucky to have met my wife and married her. I have great kids, I did a TV show, and made enough money to afford to be a jazz musician. In that way, I am really thrilled with my life. Sometimes I'm frustrated because I feel I'm not appreciated in the jazz community for how great a jazz piano player I *think* I am, my experience and everything. . . . If I get someone in the room to hear my band, me playing, if they like this kind of music, they'll love it, and that to me is success." Currently, Michael is "still trying to be a musician. . . . I feel I've made the best music ever, now that I'm well, I want to play beautiful music. I'm not trying to prove anything anymore, I don't have to be hip, I want to play music that moves me, everything has a mood, I feel I've honed in my art."

NOTES

- Determine what success means to you.
- Have patience.
- Have a positive attitude. Be pleasant to everyone you meet. (You never know who will be in a position to give you an opportunity!)
- Be professional, show up on time, be prepared.
- Realize that nothing worthwhile will come easy.
- Ignore the naysayers because they will be out in full force.
- Success leaves clues; search for them.
- Face your fears.

PART FOUR

ON PERFORMANCE ETIQUETTE

We love you madly.
—Duke Ellington

CHAPTER 11
Putting On a Performance

Are you an artist, an entertainer, a performer? It matters not what field of entertainment you are in, be it music, comedy, acting—you are in *show* business. People pay to see you, which makes it incumbent on you to put on the best performance that you can. You should be prepared, and, in my opinion, you should be presentable. Current dogma suggests that jazz is dead or dying and that musicians are choosing artistry over communication; they want to present their art without "clowning." I submit that one does not have to sacrifice one for the other. Some of the greatest jazz musicians managed to do both—Louis Armstrong, Dizzy Gillespie, and Jimmy Heath come to mind. I've seen mediocre artists who put on fun shows and really good performers who bore me to death. It's about connecting to the audience in a positive way. Think about the audience, don't talk down to us, include us with what's happening onstage, we're there to support you. We understand that the music is serious and that you are committed to your art, but there's no need to take yourselves so seriously.

Performing is what you do, so it is incumbent on you to understand *what* makes a good show. There is nothing more annoying than to go to a show and see people making it up on the fly. I've watched musicians look at their bandmates and ask, "What do you want to play now?" I have witnessed leaders ask the audience what they want to hear. The audience does not want to pay to see people rehearse onstage. Believe me, we can tell when you don't have it together. Unless you are starting out, keep in mind, folks won't pay to see you again. But you really have to be good for us to give you another chance. Fans want to see growth. With the promise of a ride home and a great evening of music, I dragged my friend Linda, who was not a fan of jazz music, to a club to see a musician whom I love and respect. He is a well-respected jazz musician who had always put on a great show each time I had seen him. I have no idea what was on his mind that night, but I knew that we were in trouble when he announced to the audience, "You look like serious jazz fans. I don't know what we are going to do, but . . ." It was not a good night of music, and to my chagrin, Linda agreed. Her comment to me, without any provocation, was, "They sounded like they were playing music for themselves." I, too, felt the same sentiment. When I asked her if she would come out with me again to a jazz club, she said, "*No!*" You can always count on Monte Croft to give a great show. "I love the show part of show business and the art. I hope to partner with good people. I've worked with good people who were inexperienced at knowing the business and how things work. Can't all be starting from scratch. Need connections. Worked with people I liked."

A great show is about pacing. Premier electric bassist, composer, and arranger Marcus Miller worked and collaborated with Miles Davis on six recordings, including the Grammy Award–winning *Tutu*. His show, Miles Davis's "Electric Miles," was outstanding. He took us on a musical journey of Miles from 1969 to 1992 that was informative, fun, and engaging. Marcus shared stories about how he came to work with Miles, how he approached writing some of the songs that he performed. It was brilliant. The interplay between the musicians was inclusive. They were playing to one another and to us at the same time. That same week I attended that show, I hosted a tribute to Nancy Wilson that was also outstanding. The balance between talk and music was perfect, it began and ended on time. No one spoke too long, they showed a short video of Nancy. We all left on a high note.

CONNECT WITH THE AUDIENCE

There is a synergy between comedy and music. For decades, comics would open shows. Gary Walker (WBGO, 88.3FM) shared a story about saxophonist Don Byron, who, when working on a duo project, said, "that is a whole other thing, a mind-set, sensitivity and rhythmic thing." To prepare, Don listened to the Grammy Award–winning American improvisational comedy duo act of Mike Nichols and Elaine May for the timing and sense of rhythm; they were two people riffing. Known for his exciting shows, Etienne Charles, too, looks to comedy for inspiration. He considers, "Entertaining is a big part of what I do. . . . I learn from how comedians talk. Comedy and music used to be related. We need to understand history. . . . I use the art of improv. . . . You want the audience to connect with *you* and the music." Though each venue has different requirements, in general he won't play songs that are too long, or boring. He won't talk after each song and will talk about originals, won't talk too long, and will "keep it funny." Further, he notes, "don't assume that people understand what you say, be clear when you speak, don't bring your personal problems onstage. It's OK to talk about world problems. . . . Most importantly, show gratitude."

Don't play the same set twice! Some people stay for both sets. Etienne reminded me of a night at Dizzy's when we went to support a young musician making his debut as a leader. Given that Dizzy's is a premier club, it was a big deal. So impressed were we with the first set, we decided to stay. To my shock, he played the same songs, in the same order. OK, jazz is improvisational, but, damn, was the second set boring. Afterward, I pulled the young man aside to tell him that he needed more material! Remember, this is show business. Think about the audience. Bassist Ron Carter gave Etienne some good advice; "You should have no more than ten to twelve songs in the book to play between two sets; have some standby tunes if the set is too short, or long." And you should include a familiar song or two. People like familiarity. It might be an original that is a hit. Christian McBride is an example of someone who covers hit songs from the 1970s, like "Car Wash."

Eric Reed is one of my favorite musicians, personally, musically, and in performance. He is a master at preparation and makes the audience feel comfortable. He opens with telling us to have a drink, he'll sound better if we do.

It's important to just be yourself and sometimes that's the worst advice you can give to some people. If people appreciate your music enough in general they can look past some things. Take Tom Harrell, for instance, his condition being what it is, he's such a phenomenal player, you just put the other thing aside. Once he takes his horn out of his mouth, he's just standing there being Tom and some people might find that difficult to understand, or to deal with it might throw you off, especially if you're experiencing it for the first time. With Keith Jarrett, you have to know that if somebody coughs he'll probably have a cow, but if you can deal with the little fit he throws, until he gets to the piano and plays you're good to go. You have to go to these performances knowing what you're getting into. Nowadays Benny Golson will talk as long as he'll play, but you want to hear Benny Golson, if he plays for thirty minutes and talk for two hours but it's worth it. As far as the real compelling entertainers, Christian McBride, Wycliffe Gordon, Roy Haynes, (the late) Roy Hargrove, Ray Brown, there's a certain kind of energy we all share or shared that we are very much aware of people and we like to hear the response and the energy from people. Keith likes absolute silence; I don't need that, I need to know folks are there. More than anything I desire for people to *know* what we're doing on the bandstand. Being able to express that I'm playing the song and how it came about. I began to include Naima, I love to acknowledge her existence, she's practically forgotten, she doesn't get talked about, which is a sad part about relationships. (I hear from women, half-jokingly—you clean up a guy and prepare him for someone else.) I like sharing these stories with people.

"I love doing projects and sharing with people." Writer Jill Nelson turned Eric on to the idea of "serial monogamy": "A relationship goes to its natural end, that it, that's how I see projects. Being able to share my experience with people, the more I play music the more I'm sharing my life with people and giving insight on why I write things and I write about people. Music is, like 'Pops' said, 'All music is folks music, have you ever seen a horse play a violin?'"

He continues, "I love audiences, I like being in the spotlight not because of my ego because I like to entertain, I like to make people laugh, sometimes I can be funny. I like to make people think, I like to celebrate people in front of people. I like people, being able to make people aware of the joy of being human, let's celebrate life, let's celebrate humanity. In the club let's just forget there's an outside, for about an hour . . ."

TO REHEARSE OR NOT TO REHEARSE

How one prepares varies from musician to musician. A sideperson must learn the music *before* the rehearsal. Rehearsal time varies among genres. Jazz musicians, in general, are not paid for their rehearsal time whereas classical musicians are, but, due to union rules, for the most part, the length of time to rehearse is limited. Pop musicians will rehearse for nine or ten hours a day. Regardless of how you prepare, it must be done. To quote cellist Ignacy Jan Paderewski, "If I don't practice for one day, I know it; if I don't practice for two days, the critics know it; if I don't practice for three days, the audience knows it." Working bands may not require regular rehearsals unless they are working on new material, but each member must be ready for each performance. Kenny Washington has worked with pianist Bill Charlap so often, along with Peter Washington on bass, that rehearsals are not necessary. Kenny says, "If one knows the music, there is no need to rehearse." He will mentally prepare, though. He says he gets "to the venue at least twenty minutes to a half hour before to relax; I do not want to be rushed."

Monte Croft loves to rehearse and finds it problematic when musicians don't make themselves available for rehearsals or show up late or when they don't want to show up for sound checks. Below is an excerpt from his Facebook page that illustrates his frustration with egotistical musicians.

> I've told cats to make sound check, and I've gotten responses like, "I don't really have anything to check,"—what? You're playing an instrument, aren't you? "That's too early"—what? Well excuse me your royal highness. "I don't need to sound check"—what? Well, I need you to sound check, it is a group, and a room.
>
> These quotes are real, and have come from stellar musicians most of you know if you've followed jazz in the last thirty years. You see, when you don't have a certain "elite" status, it doesn't matter to some cats that you're paying them—they have to somehow one-up you. It's like "I may just be a sideman, but I'm still doing better stuff than you."
>
> That's one aspect of human nature that has always irked me, and don't even mention the rehearsal thing, or dress codes. I know a cat that I'm pretty sure still bears a grudge against me because I told him he wasn't dressed appropriately to be a special guest on my gig—just to play one tune that he played on the record. He knew it was in a top club, and some video footage was being shot. I was just trying to get my thing off the ground, and the way we dressed back then was not even a question—it wasn't like it is today. Granted, it was a favor to me, but if you don't want to do something right, then just say no. Somebody gets angry with you because you responded to what you felt was disrespect. Wow. If I was on the other end of that,

I'd apologize and give the person the benefit of the doubt. You try to help people "get up," especially when everybody's young. . . . I look at my life now and think "everything is really cool—surprisingly cool even," but I would be so much further along if I hadn't had to fight so many battles with people you'd think would be in my corner.

No fan of rehearsal, Ron Carter's opinion is "one rehearsal before we go to work, whenever that is. I don't like to rehearse. I think it's a waste of time and effort, but you got to do it just to say hello to everybody." I asked, "Why is it a waste of time?" He said, "Most of the horn players want to play their brains out in rehearsal, and they have none left for the gig. Most guys don't have the music prepared for the rehearsal. Guys don't take it seriously and don't show up on time, and it kind of gets dragged out. Rehearsal space costs fifty dollars an hour. It's pretty expensive to get a good space. I have rehearsals just to make sure we have the music and that we agree that this is the right song for this title. That the changes are correct, and just again to have a quick musical review of the eighty-nine tunes I want to cover that week."

Unlike in classical music, jazz musicians tend not to be paid for rehearsals. However, the leader may pay or if the venue is large, like the Kennedy Center, paid rehearsals tend to be factored into the fee. To Ron, I asked, "Do musicians get paid for rehearsals?" "By and large, no. Jazz players don't; classical players always got paid. They make $40,000 a year, on an average. That's the low end of the scale," says Carter. Classical conductor David Randolph confirmed what Ron said regarding classical musicians getting paid for rehearsals: "Time is the enemy. A small orchestra will cost $35,000 for rehearsal and performance. There are union rules, they get ten minutes rest per hour, so you must know what you will ask for. We rehearse for the first time on Thursday for a concert on Saturday. I get first-rate musicians." The above figures are based on 2004 standards. Aaron Diehl works in both jazz and classical music: "They come from two different traditions. Orchestras are on union rules so they won't have many hours to rehearse before a performance; maybe only have one hour." Dorothy

Lawson explained, "Rules of standardized conditions are essential for groups of employees, in settings of any size. ETHEL, however, is a cooperative organization, without a boss. We discuss our conditions and make agreements among ourselves, very few of which are written into law, although we do have a contractual agreement."

DO A SET LIST—HAVE ENOUGH TUNES

You must be prepared before you present yourself. Have a set list of X number of tunes so that both sets aren't the same. If you are going to present a new arrangement, work it out *before* the gig.

Tia Fuller gained lots of insight having worked with Beyoncé: "I took lots from Bey and brought it back to jazz, like how to make set lists, integrate set lists, building interludes, speaking about songs, and doing a complete presentation. My albums are like a story/journey. Integrating lights, etc. I learned how to put a production together, how to do lights. The education was priceless including the eight hours of rehearsals that I didn't like." Regarding specifics of putting together a set list: "Don't put the same type of tune next to each other. Have a Latin, a ballad. It must have a shape; not all songs should be upbeat. As far as presentation, I learned how to introduce the band, connect verbally with the audience."

APPEARANCE/PRESENTATION

I must admit my trepidation when addressing this topic because lines between formal and casual wear have blurred. Call me "old school," but I remember when a standard dress code existed. We had our school clothes (in my case, I wore a uniform), our church clothes, party clothes, and work clothes. Every industry had a dress code; your job determined your outfit, executives/managers wore suits, women wore skirts/dresses (then pantsuits were acceptable). In the eighties and nineties, "dress-down Fridays" became a thing—though shorts and sweats were frowned upon. Those mores existed in the arts, as well. Each genre had a "look." Classical musicians wore black, if not tuxes, jazz musicians' looks are fluid, rock musicians were a bit showy, and so on. For musicians like Pat Metheny, appearance is not an issue. I have seen him perform several times, and he wears his "uniform" of jeans and a striped polo shirt. Over time, some musicians have changed their look. Before his weight loss, Chick Corea donned Hawaiian-print shirts and sneakers. Now I see him wearing suits. Miles Davis went from suits to hippie-type clothes in the 1970s. Conductor David Randolph said that he would love to not have to wear the tuxedo, but a musician must have a certain persona that the audience can relate to or aspire to. Musicians have always had an impact on fashion. Cab Calloway with his zoot suits; Dizzy Gillespie, Thelonious Monk with their berets and sunglasses. Miles Davis went from suits, to tie-dye, to pants that resembled fighter attire. We cannot overlook Janis Joplin, Jimi Hendrix, or the Beatles, the psychedelic generation of Bootsy Collins, George Clinton, and, lest we forget, the gowns of the women and the outfits of the Motown performers, or the current fashions that rappers bring to the hip-hop generation.

Today, I see that people's understanding of comfort and professional is conflated. Recently, I went to a comedy club to see a friend of mine. He was working on a show that involved four comics—two men, two women. Mind you, my friend is a *great* dresser, he has his shirts made and is meticulous. The comics were dressed casually, but I was bothered by the women's attire. The men had on jeans and suit jackets (one had a cool white Stetson hat), but both women looked as if they'd just come in from doing Saturday chores. One wore a striped sweatpants suit with a hoodie, and the other wore an unflattering jumpsuit. For fear of sounding shallow, I asked my friend if their look was common in the comedy world, because I found it distracting. His reply was that entertainers want to be "comfortable" onstage rather than look "dressed up." What baffles me is that performers don't understand that one can look professional *and* be comfortable. As he rightfully pointed out, "most people don't get that we are judged within three seconds." He also noted that the better dressed, the bigger the applause.

The same applies in the music industry. To quote the great drummer/bandleader Art Blakey, "They see you before they hear you."

Saxophonist Victor Goines dubbed me "the fashion police" because one night at Dizzy's I took it upon myself to critique what he was wearing. Years ago, I hired a trio to open for the Newark Museum gala. I thought I had made it clear to the leader what the event was. When his bass player showed up wearing a denim shirt, I grabbed his shirt to say, "This is *all* wrong." To which he replied, "I didn't know that this was a gala," and that the leader didn't tell him what the gig was. Again, perhaps it is *me* who is out of touch or shallow. My concern was that I would be, incorrectly, judged for choosing unprofessional musicians for that event.

In jazz, I've seen the pendulum swing back to a more formal dress and what is considered "casual chic." Several young men, like Aaron Diehl and Bruce Harris, are getting a reputation for being well dressed. Aaron noted that the late Roy Hargrove had set a standard as "fashion forward." Roy would don a suit and bow tie with matching sneakers. Even his casual clothes were hip. Advice from Aaron: "Be presentable. Don't be sloppy, show respect to the audience. Use common sense." In the first edition of this book, Eric Reed felt this way about the importance of dressing for performance:

> It depends. One thing that I hate when I played with Wynton was in the outside, hot festivals we'd have to wear three-piece suits. Outdoors is outdoors. Would I perform in jeans? I doubt it—I'm used to dressing up. Let me be clear: It has nothing to do with the music. It had *no* effect on music. If we were rock and roll musicians, it would be expected. The audience would be insulted if we wore tuxedos. I think the idea of wearing suits became important again in the 1980s because there was a lack of respect for jazz music. People did not give a damn about us jazz musicians—they saw us as junkies, strung out, temperamental, with a superior attitude. Music died, fusion, Miles Davis. When Wynton came in, he made the statement that this is to be taken seriously and is dignified, classy music, great music to be respected. This is how I want to be presenting

myself when I'm playing the music. What people were doing before was just trash.

Over the years, Eric has had a change of heart regarding his dress:

> For the most part, I no longer have to wear suits. The gen-
> eration I grew up in we were all suited down . . . the tie,
> the socks, we were meticulously dressed and would come
> onstage with our best vines on to see if we could outshine
> each other. It was a lot of money wasted, because I don't
> wear any of that stuff now. To me it's about comfort, I'm
> comfortable in shirt and pants, if ironed and clean, I'm
> good to go. For me, dressing more casually, I believe, puts
> the audience at ease. When I'm performing it's kind of
> informal, I like to make the music more conversational,
> I like to see myself doing lecture demos and pulling away
> from the concert scene. I love Q&A, people have ques-
> tions. On occasion I'll take questions from the audience.
> My sister thinks I've become lackadaisical and wants me
> to go back to wearing a suit. Jeans and sneakers don't
> bother me (from my sideman), but I'll tell them what I'm
> wearing but won't tell them how to dress. All I care about
> is the music happening onstage.

One night, Allan Harris left his suit at home by accident. I remember thinking that his dress was unusually casual for him, but I thought
that was deliberate. Weeks later, we talked about that night, and he
said that he was upset when he left his suit at home, but the night was
liberating for him, because he was able to relax more and be more
focused on the songs and not on his "act." Unfortunately, this does
not work for all musicians. When the audience likes you, many do
see your show more than once, so you should give them something
to look at. What performers need to remember is that your visual
presentation is part of your persona and can be a complement to your
performance, at least in the mind of the audience. In the classical

genre, all women who sing chorus or background must wear black, but the soloist can dress like a diva.

Like so many jazz musicians, Bobby Sanabria learned from the late legendary drummer Art Blakey, who was not only known for picking great musicians (many went on to lead their own bands—Wynton Marsalis played in Art's band, the Jazz Messengers). He also had a dress code, of sorts: "Don't look like shit onstage," says Bobby.

> Even Janis Joplin, Jimi Hendrix had a certain style in their dress that ended up in popular culture. In jazz, that is a lost art. Presentation is very important. Especially the tradition I represent. It is a marginalized genre, and I'm struggling to see that we get the proper respect we deserve in Latin American music, in all facets. I want to make sure the music is presented with dignity, class, and respect. The guys before me had to pay serious dues for us. I like to look good onstage. I'm known for talking to the audience. I provide "edutainment." Most of the audiences don't know much about the music. Once you speak to the audience, they are learning, and they feel relaxed.

Ron Carter is a great dresser both on- and offstage.

> You see guys who look like those rappers with the over-long clothes and stuff. People expect a certain vibe from those people. They expect a certain format, a certain attitude, a certain character, a certain carriage. I think when you walk out there as we have been, as I've always done, wearing a suit and tie, they get a different view of what they expect. For me, it's like, I'm going to work. And I am not going to work dressed as I am right now. Jeans, clogs, T-shirt—I wouldn't go like the way I'm dressed now to Birdland. You know when you're dressed like I am right now for work, people expect a different mentality.

The bandstand is my office, and I'm going to my office to work. Up until three years ago, when the offices relaxed their dressing standards on Friday, everybody wore a shirt and tie because that was the mentality of the workplace. When I worked with the Four Generations of Miles at the Blue Note with Mike Stern, George Coleman, and Jimmy Cobb, Mike Stern came to work wearing the same black jeans and black gym shoes every night. I said, "Mike, look, we're all dressed differently; everyone is wearing a sport outfit but you. You've got to find your wife or somebody to find you a sport jacket by the weekend. By Friday and Saturday, if you don't have one, I'm not going to show up." When we walk on the stage, we kind of stun people. Not to say those other guys can't play, but we have a traditional edge on them when we walk on the stage looking like that. And it happened more than once, man, we walk out there, and we get applause before we play one note—because people like the way we look. That's half the battle, getting their attention.

Women and Dress

Ladies, listen up. A double standard still exists! Yes, it's a drag, but that's our reality. We continue to be criticized by how we look, though perhaps less so in jazz. For the most part, women in jazz have it more together. Though, what I *do* see in jazz is women (too often older women) who, for some reason, feel the need to focus on "tits and ass"! One might think that being older would bring some sophistication, but *no*! There's nothing worse than seeing an older woman try to look young, as opposed to an older woman who has style and confidence without the need to show T and A! Sometimes I think it comes down to one's "classiness," but I could be wrong. In another direction, I have observed sloppy dress on women in some high school bands that blows my mind. One such band, led by a well-dressed male conductor, featured a female singer who wore sneakers, cut-out jeans, and a frumpy white blouse for a performance. When I asked him about it, he agreed that her outfit was inappropriate, but that is how young people dress. (I acknowledged that he, as a man in the era of the #MeToo movement, might be in an uncomfortable position to speak to a young student about the dress code.) Someone must have said something though, because the following year, she was properly dressed.

Unlike pop and classical musicians, female jazz instrumentalists don't have a standard "look." The dilemma facing women is how to be taken seriously as musicians without their appearance being questioned or vice versa. For women like Camille Thurman, that was an issue. She and Tia Fuller have worked in both jazz and pop/R&B; Camille was a member of Black Girls Rock (for four years), and Tia was in Beyoncé's bands. Camille understands the visual demands of each:

> Sexism still exists. In R&B how women look is a prob-
> lem. They pressure you to lose weight, move you to the
> side of the stage. It's about how you look, sounding
> good is a plus. You have to do the same thing every
> night and the same time, again, it's how you look. We
> have to dance in heels and look cute, show skin and still
> be able to play. . . . Jazz doesn't have the direct pres-
> sure, but you can still be judged. I didn't have an image
> at first. I looked to other women of color who were
> out front. Again, I looked to my sisters for direction.
> You can control your own image and don't have to put
> skin out like in R&B. If you put out sexy, that's what
> you'll have to give them. Don't rely on the sex appeal.
> Instrumentalists vs. vocal—epitome of being sexy—but
> not one [look] for an instrumentalist. I still feel like a
> youngun . . . you can still be young at forty!

Tia Fuller bemoaned the difference between those two worlds. "You don't have to know anything about the instrument and had to have a look that can be defined and refined. Catty [Rodriquez] had just had a baby and had gained some weight. . . . They wanted a look, same height, different body types (had to have an endearing quality about yourself, too). Camille had subbed for her but wasn't chosen to replace her." She alluded to the possibility that Camille didn't get the job because of her height.

NOTES

- Gospel concerts tend to be *loud*. Why?
- Don't eat a big meal before a gig, don't drink until after a gig. Don't overuse the guest list. The bandleader must enforce that.
- Don't program long sets.
- Have X number of songs for two sets and one encore.
- Keep emotions in check.

CHAPTER 12

The Dos and Don'ts of Performing

In the previous chapter, I focused on the elements that comprise a good performance. I established that you must connect positively with the audience and make your shows interesting *and* fun. Look good and sound good. Equally important, artists should pay as close attention to what *not* to do in performing. Each genre has its own standard of what is and is not accepted. For example, tardiness is OK in the pop world—I have never gone to see Stevie Wonder and have him be on time *and* his shows always run long. Hey, it's Stevie, his shows are amazing and worth the wait. If you are notorious for tardiness, you'd better give a great show! Needless to say, if you are on a bill with other groups, don't go long. Remember, if you are doing more than one set at a venue, don't run late because they have to prepare the house for the next set. Think of the staff and the audience that is waiting in line to see you.

BE ON TIME

"Tardiness is never acceptable!" says Eric Reed. "Ninety-eight percent of the time, I'm early; I learned that from Jeff Clayton. Showing up at three o'clock for a three o'clock rehearsal is late. To be early is to be on time, to be on time is to be late, and to be late is not acceptable. You are not ready to play if you show up at three o'clock and have to set up your instrument. Keeping people waiting for you sets a bad tone and is inconsiderate and impolite."

Ron Carter agreed: "Don't be late, and don't play the set too long. Especially when you have two groups (a double bill at a club). The club has to clear out those people. And until they make that changeover, they're going to lose money. They're going to lose when bands have gone off the schedule. The income for the clubs has taken a big dip because they can't get the people in and out for the second or the third show, or the second or third band. Oh, yeah, that's a big issue." This is also an issue in classical music. David Randolph said they "don't look kindly on lateness." Dorothy Lawson confirmed this when I asked if tardiness was not accepted: "It just won't work."

BE COOL

We all have good and bad days, but once we get in front of people, it is our job to minimize our problems. My observations are those of a person who's been to countless performances.

As a musician, it is in your best interest to make the audience feel comfortable with what you are presenting. They take their cues from you. If you have confidence, they will feel confident; if you are involved and inspired, they will be, too. Also, if you make a mistake, find a way to correct it without stopping the show. Ella Fitzgerald won a Grammy for her performance of "Mack the Knife" where she forgot the words to the song and improvised the lyrics. I will always remember a concert where a singer came out, started in the wrong key or place, and told the band to stop and start again. The leader looked on in horror and so did the audience. Had she not stopped the band, I would not even have noticed that something was wrong. There is no need to call attention to problems. I know how frustrating it is when the sound and light crew are not good, but it's best to not call them out from the stage when they mess up. I saw a well-known singer chastise the light man. In between songs, she told him to stop following her and quipped, "I feel like I'm in Stalag 13." As a result, he continued to do what he'd been doing as if to say, "F you." She was also boring as heck. Most of the people sitting in my row began to exit in unison. My friends and I were about to join them and leave, too, but then she began to sing a familiar song, so we remained in our seats, but the show went downhill from there. Still, years later, when I meet people who were at that concert, we all agree that we would not see her again. At some point, my friend, Sam, encouraged his friends to see her. After the show, his friends asked him what *he* had seen in her, and they, too, vowed to never pay to see her again.

Many master musicians, like Art Blakey, said to keep your personal life off the bandstand. It's fine to share things happening in your life without detracting from the show. Dorothy Lawson talked openly for the first time about a bad performance experience that she had by letting a relationship interfere:

> There was a recital at Juilliard. It was my first doctoral recital, and it was a disaster, and I was unprepared. I have to admit that I was going through a tumultuous and difficult relationship, and I could not see myself beyond that, and it had an impact on my judgment. It was a lesson for me to try to forgive myself for being human. What I have been able to do: one, try to forgive myself and recognize, in general, that what the audience receives from my music is not entirely what I intend, anyway. Even if you are in great shape and play what you wanted, the audience will take away what resonates for them, and it might not be about you. I try hard not to drag feelings of criticism or disappointment into the dealing with the audience or other musicians. They each have their own needs to deal with.

PACING SETS

It's easy to get wrapped up in a set. Bobby Sanabria says, "I used to play too long. I was in the moment and programmed too much music in the set, but I've learned over the years. I want my sets to be like a good play and have a logical progression. There is always something spiritual. I play a spiritual song at the beginning to set the tone and separate myself from other leaders. Also, the soloists are featured in different settings, [and my sets are] not formulaic."

AUDIENCE ENGAGEMENT

A bad show is when twenty minutes feels like one hour has passed. I have been to many where I've felt if I *had* paid to get in, I would have been more unhappy. Tribute shows tend to be the most uninspiring. If you are performing the music of someone, please include some of their hits. Another turnoff is to talk after each tune. Etienne Charles gets it:

> I don't talk after each tune. I'll play two or three back to back, at the top of the set, then I'll say something, introduce the musicians, talk about my original tunes—tell where they came from. It helps you connect with the audience. I always thank the presenter and the audience and show gratitude. Things take away from a show—if the songs are too long, the audience can feel that. If the song is boring, allow a drum solo. Have some standby tunes, know what tune you'll cut. Know that the last tune can be the encore. Cannonball Adderley said that his sets were "50 percent of what the audience wants to hear and 50 percent of what I want them to hear."

It's about show business. Allan Harris learned from comics:

> **Number one:** Study the audience before you go onstage. One must be in sync with what is going on outside. You are not just showing off your craft; *you are an entertainer.* You have to make them feel comfortable. Once you have them, you can take them anywhere you want to go. I did twenty

shows with the late comedian Alan King, and he'd write down notes on what I had to do. For example, *don't say*, *"How yawl doin'?"* Get out, sing, have a theme. Make sure the band is on the same page as you; be in sync. **Number two:** Do not do anything you are not comfortable with; it will always bite you in the butt. Alan scratched ten songs out of my repertoire, *my show*, ten songs out of twenty— he was brutal! Tony Bennett did the same thing to me; he, too, asked, "Why are you doing this song?" *Scratch!* It was a rude awakening. By show number sixteen, I was rolling.

Humor helps. Eric Reed is also great with the audience: "To engage the audience, I might act like I don't remember what I played, and they will shout out the tunes. A dead audience drains me to no end, which is why I always begin by telling them that it's OK to enjoy the music. Back in the day, people danced to the music; I tell them it's OK to interact with us, make some noise." I thank Eric for making that observation, because somewhere along the way a "silent policy" found its way into jazz clubs. Jazz used to be dance music and fun. Yes, it is distracting if people are carrying on a conversation during a show, but the audience should be able to express, verbally or otherwise, their appreciation.

The interplay between jazz and gospel audiences is vast. Gospel folks go ready to be inspired and engaging. My issue with those concerts is that no matter the size of the venue, their shows tend to be way too loud! I always look forward to attending a Richard Smallwood show, because he is always uplifting. He says,

> In performance, the connection has to be there with the audience. It is important to set up a rapport. They must feel that you are warm and open with them, not that you are oblivious to who they are or what they are doing. To get a good performance, the artist has to flow between the audience, and the artist has to be friendly, to be sensitive. I could not approach an audience in Norway the same way

as a church audience on Sunday morning. My musicians are on pins and needles because they don't know where I'll go.

Not your "typical" classical musician who has a reputation for being stoic onstage, Dorothy Lawson is very physical, and she smiles a lot; her enthusiasm is infectious. She says, "There is nothing universal about it, but it's the way I feel most authentic. I feel physical about the rhythm, and I feel most in contact when I allow that to come through. I smile because I'm so grateful that the audience is there. I really come to feel that the performers are the lucky ones who are being subsidized by the audience to actually develop the skill that it takes to do the stuff themselves. It is such a pleasure to be an artist, to be a musician." As a coleader of the group ETHEL, she has found kindred spirits: "The other thing, one of the funny things, about ETHEL, we are all *very* physical and very engaged with the audience in that way. When we met, we all felt, *at last!* We all experienced being too much for other people, moving too much or talking about whatever on the other hand. We tailor ourselves to work well with other people."

A PERFORMANCE OR A REVIEW?

When your name is on the marquee, people are paying to see you, so don't load the show with numerous special guests. Singers are notorious for this. It's as if they need validation. The minute you brag about *who* is in your band for the evening, I intuit that you're not secure about yourself and lean on the band to make *you* sound better. Too many folks sitting in or being featured can turn your set into a variety show (that may be your goal). Do you want people walking away thinking about how much they enjoyed you, or your special guests? Understand the performance venue. I've seen musicians allow young relatives to do a tune or two. Before you highlight the young person, make sure that they can perform on a high level.

SIDEPERSON, TAKE NOTE

Remember that you are a part of the show. What you do is equally important to the leader. Kenny Washington has to think about his drum solos. I remind him how people claim to hate drum solos.

> I always think about the melody. I learned that from Max Roach. The drummer must know the tune, the form, like everyone else in the bandstand. Also, dynamics. The worst drum solos are where guys play at one level and loud and long. That's why people don't dig drum solos. Most people can get into jazz, but the problem is nowadays the stuff is sad. Folks go hear people who are sad and will say, apologetically, they did not understand it. Their guts tell them it is not happening, but they listen to critics who praise the music, so they think they don't understand it and put themselves down. If the music is done right, people don't have to understand it; they feel it. The real pros will be working, one way or another. Like Bill Charlap. That is a hell of a band. Audiences are not stupid. They don't have to know anything about jazz to like the music. That's the way jazz was years ago. Charlap plays the American Songbook, and he is getting younger audiences, and people come back. The sets are well paced, songs don't go on too long, so I'm curious to see what happens to the band, now that Tommy Flanagan is dead.

NOTES

- Performer checklist:
  1. Be sensitive; get to know your audience. Feel their energy.
  2. Be prepared; know the songs.
  3. Regarding demeanor, look like you want to be onstage. Stand up straight.
  4. Respect your fellow musicians. Encourage them during their solos.
  5. Cultivate an image; dress appropriately.
  6. Don't bore the audience with long or meaningless solos.
  7. Don't talk down to the audience.
  8. Don't be drunk or high.
- Do not talk after each tune.
- Have variety; songs should have different tempos.
- Feature each musician in some way. Avoid the usual jazz set with head, solo, head . . .
- Read the room and change the set order if the audience isn't engaged.
- Sideperson: Don't abuse the guest list; it goes against the leader's tab.

CHAPTER 13

Jam Sessions

A jam session is a somewhat informal musical event where musicians go to get work experience, work on some material, and check out players on the scene. In the late 1930s, Henry Minton, the first black delegate to the American Federation of Musicians Local 802, and original owner of Minton's Playhouse, started holding regular Monday-night sessions because that was the night most musicians were off. Union rules prohibited musicians from playing those sessions, but because of his union ties, they looked the other way. According to Ralph Ellison, Minton's Playhouse provided "a retreat, a homogeneous community where a collectivity of common experience could find continuity and meaningful expression." Minton hired Teddy Hill to put together a house band that included Thelonious Monk, Kenny Clarke, and Joe Guy. It attracted frequent guests like Dizzy Gillespie and Charlie Christian. Minton's played an important role in the evolution of swing to bebop by inspiring the next generation to come and jam with the likes of Coleman Hawkins, Lester Young, and Roy Eldridge. Miles Davis recalled his time hanging there:

> On Monday nights at Minton's, Bird and Dizzy would
> come in to jam, so you'd have a thousand [players] up

there trying to get in so they could listen to and play with Bird and Dizzy. But most of the musicians in the know didn't even think about playing when Bird and Dizzy came to jam. We would just sit out in the audience, to listen and learn.

Through the years, Minton's became so popular the house band began to develop ways of weeding out less skilled musicians who wanted to sit in. Musicians had to audition before getting on the bandstand. They'd take them in the kitchen, make them play a few tunes to see if they could pass the muster. Eddie "Lockjaw" Davis is legendary for running jam (or cutting) sessions. His stage was where the wheat was separated from the chaff; if you couldn't play or keep up, you'd be told to leave the stage. They had rules. No one cared if your feelings got hurt if you were not allowed to sit in or were kicked off the stage. Jam sessions have lost some appeal for both the musicians and the audience. I find myself in frequent conversations with musicians who share their frustration about the current jam session scene. There was a time when I looked forward to attending them. Certain venues, like St. Nick's Pub or the Lenox Lounge (both no longer in existence), drew a cross section of musicians of all ages; you never knew who would show up to sit in. Roy Hargrove was great about supporting the scene. He was a frequent guest and passed on his knowledge to the younger set. His loss will be felt for a long time.

Aaron Diehl is adamant that musicians learn jam session rules:

> Don't play too long on solos! Maybe wait to the next tune if you play too long. [To the leaders] Think of a jam session as if you're doing a set. Put a ballad in them, change the tempos. Horns, piano, bass, then drums is boring and why people don't like to listen to jam sessions. It's still for the listening public. The leader may sit at the bar instead of being a part of the session. Roy Hargrove used to conduct the jam sessions and was the ringleader and would teach tunes on the stand and run interference if someone

played too long or wasn't playing the changes. Roy tried to galvanize young musicians who played.

Although it's rare that I focus on people's dress at jam sessions, I must admit that I *do* make visual judgements. You may think that it's unfair to be judged by your appearance, but that's reality. If you want to be a professional, you should look like one. Below is a Facebook exchange regarding jam sessions' dress taken from Monte Croft's timeline that is revealing:

Monte Croft: Jazz is coming out of a student environment, today, and most of them feel it's all about the music, and not at all about how we look, which is a sea change for jazz music. So many "older" cats have acquiesced to this aesthetic, that it's just what's happening today. This makes me "the rebel"—sweet, how that worked out. I just watched a live feed of a jam session, and they sound really good to be so young, but they look like they don't give a damn. Jeans, sneakers, sweats, etc. Granted, it's a jam session, but it's such a major change from when we came up. The thought of going to a major NYC club to attend a session, hosted by an established older artist, in sweats and sneakers? They need to at least know that's a relatively new phenomenon, and some of us are really not feeling that. We're not accorded the respect that was given to our predecessors when they were our age, so younger folks would rather argue, or dismiss the notion of a dress code. There was a time when clubs would not let you in at all, in sweats, jeans, and sneakers. Everybody gets a vote, that's my vote.

Commenter A: I have a question since I'm not from that time. And I'm asking this from a humble righteous place. I was raised Old School and still believe, when you perform, dress to impress . . . my question is about dressing up at jam sessions. The times have changed, and in society on average, [for] most business people, pastors, etc., "dress up" is a button down, some fly sneakers, and a blazer. Getting back to my question, do you feel it's rude or disrespectful to the culture to not be decked out at a jam session?

Monte Croft: I look at it like this, our environment is what WE make it, be it our homes, our neighborhoods, our gathering places, etc. More specifically to your question, younger people seem to look at things in extremes. I might suggest being "presentable," and your response might be "he wants to see us decked out," when that is not necessarily true. I had a young guy go in on me because he said he didn't want to wear suits, but he failed to realize I never suggested he wear suits. He saw my suits and made that assumption. I believe whenever you're onstage, before the people, some thought should go into your visual presentation. If you look the same way in rehearsal as you do in a PUBLIC jam session, perhaps you might want to consider an adjustment. We all know times have changed—perhaps more than you even realize. Musicians used to dress up for flights and recording sessions; those days are gone, but check this out. I did a record date with Brian Blade last year, and he informed us that one day a photographer would be there. I'm usually totally casual in the studio, but when I got that information I decided for that day I would wear a jacket with my jeans, and a cap I thought was fly—still had on sneakers. Just that simple thought process lifted my look up—I didn't think "oh, I have to wear a suit now." I don't live in a vacuum; I see the same things you see. I'm just trying to give the younger folks something to chew on. This thing is what WE make it. Your vote has the same weight as mine.

Commenter B: Hip-hop has a look, country has a look, rock and roll has a look—jazz is indecisive, or we

155

want so badly to be down we adopt the hip-hop thing. I'm like, but what is the "jazz look" today?

Commenter C: It's about holding the bandstand/stage as special and always having your stage persona. Stage wear can be written off on your taxes!! I have things that I wear on stage that I don't wear every day or at jam sessions. They are supposed to be a spontaneous event. But I always try to look like an artist when I leave home. I'm old school in that way. Be it a scarf, a jacket, shoes, shirt, etc., we are special and should always present ourselves as such. "They see you before they hear you." Not my words. Peace!! Onward and upward.

For years, saxophonist Mike Lee has been conducting jam sessions at various clubs. With this younger generation, he has watched them deteriorate. In a recent post from his online newsletter, he addressed his concerns:

Most jazz musicians have attended many jam sessions. Few of us have hosted a recurring jam session over a long time period. Here are some things I'd like you to consider:

Hosting is hard. There are many points of consideration when trying [to] run a jam session that might not ever cross the mind of the average session attendee. It is important to remain a good positive rapport with the musicians you hire for the house band, with the regular fans, with younger participating musicians, with established/known musicians who might stop through, and with the servers, bartenders, and owner of the venue. Each of these groups might have a different set of needs and agendas. I often joke that the trick is not to try to please everyone, but just to decide who you're going to piss off tonight. The understanding of the chemistry and interdependence of each of these categories of people is what sets a good jam session apart from a great one.

I want you to succeed. I want you to have a great musical and social experience which rewards your love for the music and challenges you to increase your skills and understanding of the music. Try to understand if things don't exactly as you hoped this week. There might be 600 other considerations I'm juggling at that moment.

I'm your host. Please say hello and goodbye. It's courteous and helps me know if I'm on the right track providing a valuable event.

Competition has its place. Most of the greatest musicians had storied "battles" that helped create their legend. These battles often happened at jam sessions. If you feel "defeated" or "cut"—come back next week and reclaim your stake.

Buy something. The venue is providing the scene and the lights and electricity. They are counting on your business. An appetizer and a soda go well with a late night set.

It's cool to let me know you'd like someday to play in the house band, but it often puts me in an awkward place. I have a fairly regular rotation of players I use and I have spent a lot of time and energy cultivating a nice network of professionals whom I can count on for many reasons. Throwing a new cat into the mix isn't always as easy as it seems. It's not that you're not KILLING IT!, but it's not as easy as it seems.

It's cool to come and hang out and listen to all the players without sitting in. I feel so many people are so apprehensive about sitting in that they'd rather sit home than come participate as listeners. But you can gain a lot of information just observing.

Play short—it's a winning formula. Play one less chorus than you think and people will love you.

Young cats—please forgive me when I forget your name or don't recognize you. I meet 100 new people every week. And you grew a beard or lost 50 pounds. It can throw me off![1]

NOTES

- Observe the rules.
- Don't cop an attitude if you aren't called to sit in.
- Get to know the leader.
- Develop a rapport with other musicians.

---

1   © 2019 by Mike Lee. Reprinted here with permission from saxophonist Mike Lee. Originally appeared in online newsletter: Mike Lee, "Secrets from a Jam Session Leader," *Mike Lee*, April 22, 2019, https://mikeleejazz.com/2019/04/22/secrets-from-a-jam-session-leader/.

PART FIVE
ON THE BUSINESS

Show business is not the easiest thing to get into,
but if that's what you want, you've got to stick with it.
There have been thrills and chills and ups and downs ever
since I've been in show business. It never stops.
—Sarah Vaughan

CHAPTER 14

Self-Promotion, Presentation, and Social Media

Synergy between self-promotion and etiquette is undeniable. The Internet has negatively impacted our lives in how we communicate with one another and how we conduct business.

Growing up, manners mattered. We were taught how to greet people, encouraged not to brag, to look people in the eyes when speaking, and to know how to listen. Learn how to promote yourself and when *not* to promote yourself. Mika Karlsson said,

> Don't always go asking for things. Learn how to be a nice person, in general—that's a skill that people don't learn in school. People usually learn the opposite. Learn how to not always sell yourself. You've seen people at concerts who walk up to musicians or the conductor after the concert wanting something, right away. How about saying something like "That was an amazing concert"? I've been to so many classical music concerts where musicians walk up to composers with their business cards out. Something just happened here! [in reference to the concert] Learn social graces.

Learn to follow cues! When conversing, pay attention to how you are being received. Is the other person listening? Do you notice the distant stare—what my friend Brian Delp calls MEGO (my eyes glaze over)? I encounter so many self-promoters whose conversations go like this:

> **THEM:** How's it going?
> **ME:** I'm well, thanks. How are you?
> **THEM:** I've been here, there, working here and there, on my CD . . . blah, blah, blah. Oh, I'll send you a copy of my new CD . . .
> **ME:** [While they're talking, MEGO.] . . . OK, gotta run, good to see you.

While I was working on the first edition of this book, Ron Carter said to me, "We're all here trying to play the same twelve notes . . ." Getting heard is a universal reality to musicians, as well. And, *yes*, self-promotion can be hard. I must admit I often encounter musicians who seem to have *no* trouble with promotion. However, I wish some of them would spend more time working on their craft than pushing their gigs.

WEBSITES

You are judged by your presentation both online and off-line. In addition to a social media presence, you should have an up-to-date website. As a radio personality and a festival curator, I have to look at websites and am astounded by how user-unfriendly so many are. Artists tend to be more concerned with the "look" instead of its function. Before you design your website, apply the KISS (Keep It Simple, Stupid) principle. Consider the users' needs and experience. I find many musician websites difficult to read. The background color is black. They choose a fancy font and red, yellow, or white text. Their home pages are way too busy with photos and text. Dropdown menu tabs are confusing due to their use of euphemisms for something simple like "Biography." *Please* make sure that your bio has a download option. I'm all for creativity, but not at the expense of user content. All sites should include these features:

- A long *and* short bio for promo purposes (we don't have time to extract basic information from your long bio).
- High-resolution photos that can be easily downloaded.
- Keep your gig schedule current.
- Have some videos of your performances.
- Please don't have sound blasting when we click on your home page, or make us search for the button to turn it off.
- Link your favorite radio stations to your site (we're a community, after all).
- Show all contact information.

SOCIAL MEDIA

"[It's] a 'necessary evil,'" says Mika Karlsson, "we can't opt out, now I stopped sending out emails." If used properly, social media is a tool that allows you to promote your careers. Initially, many eyed social media with suspicion (and still do) because it appeared to invade privacy (it does). Social media has given everyone a platform to expose the intricacies of their lives and thoughts with the world. My colleague Awilda Rivera, former WBGO on-air host and social media consultant, was one of the first to embrace Facebook. On her urging, I reluctantly signed up but barely used it and did not post a profile photo; I just wasn't into it, didn't see the need! She, on the other hand, embraced social media from the beginning. I marveled at her enthusiasm to learn about @ signs and hashtags. Awilda discovered effective ways to use it to promote *Evening Jazz* and WBGO.

Social media is about branding *you*; it is similar to product branding, except you are the brand. Before you tell the world, "Here I am," you have to see yourself as the product—you are "selling" yourself. As with any product, you are competing for space and attention. How you differentiate yourself in the market—the industry—is key. As "they" say, "It's rough out here." Of all the marketing tools, social media is the most cost-effective yet can be time consuming.

Awilda Rivera works with clients of varied interests. She notes, "Though Facebook, Twitter, and Instagram are the three major platforms, musicians need a YouTube platform, as well. The more content you have, the more people will look you up." The more you publish, the better off you are. "People are visually inclined and the reason why you should consider posting a one-minute clip on Instagram," says Awilda. This is your career, choose wisely and work it.

Facebook

This has become a platform for the older generation; people under thirty have been stepping away from it. Awilda suggests, "FB is best used to promote big events such as a CD release party, book tour, and more event media. Stick to one page. Multiple pages can be confusing and make it difficult for you to be found. You're better off with a personal page because your fans like to interact with you."

Be cognizant of what you post. I understand the need to vent, but how you present yourself on social media should be an extension of your brand. Do you really want radio people to know how much you don't like them and what/who they spin? Do you want the industry to view you as angry and bitter? A presenter might think twice before hiring a musician who spends his/her time blaming others for their lack of work. I've seen musicians list reasons (the color of their skin, their age, and/or their sex) they perceive for not getting hired. Unless the presenter tells you why they *won't* hire you, don't assume you know the reason. Conversely, I've seen musicians share negative experiences that are instructive. Jeremy Pelt is an example of someone who uses Facebook well. He offers insights that foster dialogue. Below is one such post.

> **Jeremy Pelt:** Shareable thought today: Fellow musicians! If I may be avuncular: If you're REALLY trying to be out here working with your band, you gotta shed

your business chops JUST as much as your instrumental chops. Tours just don't magically happen. You gotta put in that work and get used to adversity, cause it happens at EVERY level.

Commenter A: Where do I learn those skills?

Jeremy Pelt: Well, the way I learned them was by observing others. I had great role models that knew how to hustle those gigs. Cats like Lonnie Plaxico, Ralph Peterson Jr., Vincent Herring, and Joris Dudli (Austrian drummer).

Commenter B: Personally self promotion is the hardest part of the music biz.

Commenter C: Thank you for sharing. I spent my entire day today reaching out to festivals and summer music concert series in an effort to create playing opportunities and expand. I encountered a particularly rude "gatekeeper" out of Atlanta that really pissed me off. This process is always a struggle and find encouragement that it's a battle in which we all share.

Twitter

Twitter is a more news-based platform that attracts R&B, pop, and hip-hop artists. It supports follower interaction but is not as user-friendly as FB. Don't shy away from posting video on Twitter. From DIYmusician.com: "Twitter has no qualms about live links on its platform. In fact, most Twitter feeds are almost entirely external links!"

Instagram

This platform is image-based, which gives you a wider reach to fans and other sites. The "story" feature also allows you to communicate directly with your audience. Awilda says, "looking at the trends, watching other posts, on Instagram, I see that people don't seem as compelled to follow up like they tend to do on FB, they don't even go back to that page, they don't have to." Also, learn to make use of hashtags. You will connect with so many beyond your immediate sphere. For example, she said, "On Instagram I follow people who foster animals, it's a big thing, so that's how organizations that foster get donations, it has a further reach then FB ever had. Folks use more hashtags on Instagram than on FB. Think beyond your followers!" To illustrate the good use of hashtags is this post from Aaron Diehl (photo cropped out):

♡ ♀ ⊽   • • • •   ⊓

🔵 Liked by **maxxmyrick** and **30 others**

jazzygirlrockin Repost from @artimacypodcast - Tune into #artimacypodcast on @dcradiohd TONIGHT from 8-10p ET as I chat with Jazz pianist @aaronjdiehl! I'll also talk to @wammiesdc nominees @boomscat, and @24goldenchild of @themusicianship all about WAMMIE weekend! Listen online at wwwdcradio.gov. -
.

#AaronDiehl #BOOMscat #WAMMIES #TheMusicianShip #JessicaTeachey #Artimacy #podcast # #dcradiohd #womenonair #womeninradio #radiochick

BUSINESS ETIQUETTE

How you interact in any industry environment may have an impact on your career. You should be aware that you never know *who* is around you. Though it may not be your intent, you might dismiss a stranger who turns out to be the person who could help you. First impressions are lasting. British writer Andrew Grant is famous for saying, "You never get a second chance to make a first impression." Best-selling author Malcolm Gladwell said, "We don't know where our first impressions come from or precisely what they mean, so we don't always appreciate their fragility." The "dis" happens in *all* industries. I have been a witness to it and have experienced it. A friend of mine, a black woman, is an executive for a division of one of the major networks. She took me to a network reception with few black folks in attendance. We tried to strike up a conversation with a "brother," but he blew us off. Later that evening, another executive introduced *her* to him—the look on his face was shock—he smiled then wanted to talk, but it was too late. Another example is that of a friend who sat next to a very prominent TV commentator (I was shocked that he wasn't seated at a table out of sight, so I guess he wanted to be seen) at a crowded, popular restaurant. Before she commented on what he had ordered, not recognizing him, she asked if he was an actor. He was taken aback at her lack of recognition and became a bit rude. When he told her where he worked, she told him that her nephew also works there but didn't know in what department. As it turned out, her nephew is *his* boss! I'll never forget the time that I went to see a performer for the first time. I happened to sit at the bar, next to the pianist. Without identifying myself, I tried to strike up a conversation with him. He barely responded, then picked up his phone to carry on a text conversation before abruptly getting up. To be fair, I didn't judge him for that; after all, I am guilty of texting in public. I had to leave before the set was over. On my way out, the musician announced me. He looked up from the keyboard, surprised yet smiling as if we had had a pleasant meeting earlier. At the bar I was a stranger, and he had shown no interest in engaging, but he might have had lots on his mind. Again, you never know who you're talking to you, so you should always be polite to strangers, especially in an industry setting.

We tend to focus on *how/when* to promote, but less on when *not* to promote. Some take any gathering as an opportunity to be noticed; there is a time and a place. It shows poor taste to go to a function or performance with your flyers in hand and not get permission to distribute them or leave them on the table. And equally egregious is when those same people will ignore that host and surreptitiously hand them out in the crowd. Funerals are high on my list of places to not self-promote. It's offensive—not a good look. Two funerals stand out. One was for a famous jazz musician whose funeral was held at a prominent Baptist church in Harlem. The church was packed with musicians, politicians, and media glitterati. After the service, as we streamed out into the street, greeting friends, a musician (not well respected, and casually dressed as if he'd not attended the funeral) walked through the crowd handing out his flyers promoting some club he was booking. I attended another funeral that was embarrassing. When they asked people to speak on behalf of our dearly departed, the first person to speak said a few words about him, then told us that she had to go to her gig, where it was, and that she would dedicate her show to him. She opened the floodgates; those who followed her did the same.

I suggest that you exercise discretion before you approach industry people. Avoid giving *unsolicited* CDs and flyers. Once a gentleman came to a lecture I was giving. Minutes before I began my talk, he came to the table, handed me a folder with music and promotion material of someone I didn't know. He then asked me to *call* him to discuss. Be professional, mail your material or ask *if* they want what you are handing out. I've been told, "If I'd known that you'd be here, I'd have brought my [fill in the blank]. Why should I mail it, I see you now!" There was a time that I carried a *small* purse to avoid having to take CDs musicians tried to thrust upon me. It's mindboggling how rude folks can be when I'm not receptive to taking their CDs'. A glaring example of insensitivity occurred when I was the emcee for a show that had multiple moving parts that included an award section, and each set featured different musicians. One of the musicians handed me his CD. I asked him to mail it. He looked offended and said, "My reps have sent CDs, but I see you *now*." To avoid an argument, I took it. Moments later, he pointed out a comment on the front sticker. (Not good to place it on the wrap that will be tossed when you open it, but I digress.) I cut him off midsentence by saying, "I can't talk about this now, I'm working." He didn't seem concerned that he was interrupting my job. At the end of the evening, another musician handed me *his* CD. Last, don't be lazy, when I ask you to send material to me at the station, don't ask me for the address and don't ask me for emails of other station personnel; go to the website and look it up.

THE ROLE OF RADIO

Is terrestrial radio becoming extinct? How does radio impact you? Does your music fit the format of the station? What differentiates terrestrial radio from streaming? Know the difference. You should know the general idea of the inner workings of the stations, who makes the decisions about putting your music in the mix, who arranges interviews, etc. There is a thin line between being aggressive and being annoying. Gary Walker, music director and announcer at WBGO, has a problem talking to musicians and/or their reps about their music: "I talk to a lot of artists on the phone, and the majority of them don't have a clue about their careers. They are great musicians, but they don't have a clue otherwise. I won't allow people to waste my time twice. It does not matter who contacts me regarding the artist, but I quickly find out if they know what they are talking about, I'll ask them to tell me something about the CD, such as what tracks stand out and why."

So disconnected are some musicians with reps, they don't know when or if their CDs are at the station. For those who can afford to hire a radio rep, you should check with them to see if and by whom your CD is spinning. I was shocked to get an email from a well-established musician, alerting me to her new release (it had been in WBGO for over a month, and I'd already selected tunes during my shifts) and asking me to spin it. Derrick Lucas, music director, announcer, and account executive at Jazz 90.1, is adamant that musicians should:

> Create friendships/relationships with the folks who play your music. At eighty-four years of age, Houston Person still calls me when he puts out a new record, or is a side-man on a new project. He calls the DJs who play his music, knows their families and who they are. . . . If you don't have time to listen, OK, but find out who's playing your music. You'd be surprised at how many musicians don't know who plays their music. If you're an artist and don't listen, find out what station is playing your music, make sure you have that station's link on your website. Do you help them fund-raise? Do you help us? Understand who takes care of whom.

Airplay

The impact of classical radio and emerging recording artists is not as strong as that between musicians and jazz stations.

Not much new music is played. Terrence McKnight of WQXR explained:

> In the standard repertoire of classical and romantic music, music of the twentieth century is still considered new music. . . . Beyond 1950, like bebop those composers started to get outside of norms of form and tonality, started writing atonal music and the attitude changed. Like bebop musicians, who took on an attitude similar to that of classical composers in the '40s and '50s, they didn't care what the audience liked. Some would say if they like it it must be bad. . . . Living composers are hard to put on the air. We had to make a case for us to play Philip Glass and Steven Reich—they're in their eighties now. The rotation is 90 percent standard classical, 10 percent new. New artists on the scene, in their twenties and thirties, are playing the standard repertoire to meet the needs of contemporary artists who have a digital (streaming) channel dedicated to "new sounds." Thus, "reaching younger audiences is more of a digital function." Radio stations utilize online tools to try to convert audiences to terrestrial radio. "You'll see articles online that might appeal to younger people. You'll see YouTube clips or our own videos and hope they'll convert to radio because we're listener supported. We raise a good percent of revenue from listeners who sign up during the pledge drive."

Both WBGO and Jazz 90.1 are public radio stations and rely on audience/listener support. The lion's share of operating funds come from the listeners. As purveyors of jazz, the bulk of music presented is classic music. During a twenty-four-hour cycle at WBGO, the ratio of new to classic is 25 percent to 75 percent, and at Jazz 90.1 it's 30 percent to 70 percent. At any given time, WBGO has over one hundred new releases. Out of nine tunes an hour, two or three are new. The music is programmed by the announcer, unlike satellite radio. Therefore, I suggest that you reach out to announcers and make a case for them to spin your recording.

What's Your Story?

Before Gary Walker decides which new music he places in the studio, he takes into consideration the fact that WBGO is "limited by the amount of space in a broadcast hour. In that hour we focus on classic, recurrent, players who appear in the area and are familiar to the audience who live in this area." WBGO is not a local jazz station, per se. Due to the Internet, it broadcasts around the world. If you are a musician who lives outside of the local area, one way to get noticed is to have a story. He continues,

> We're the jazz station for people in Munich, in Florida, Minnesota, during the fund drive we hear from people all over the world. We're lucky, we're in the jazz capital of the world. The energy that causes jazz to thrive is here. Because of all these platforms, we're able to spread the word all over the world. Unfortunately, it means that because there are players all over, who are very good and saying some interesting things, you won't find any more than you do around here. The reason why I put Gayelynn McKinney in rotation is that she's part of a legacy that you can tie into when you play her recordings. Sorry, "Jo Schmo" from Detroit doesn't say as much as you can say about her, that she comes from this family. It's a story and how she came to the music that has incredible amount of depth to it.

As long as I've been on the radio, musicians have complained to me about *not* getting their music placed in the library (new release bin). Keep in mind, radio is "theater of the mind," so you should think about the listener experience, how to make a connection. Gary explains,

You're trying to establish familiarity. The problem is people who have come before us have made jazz such a severe, academic experience. That's not what the impetus should be. It should be familiarity and how easy it is to enjoy the world of jazz. And the same relationship should exist with the musicians who make this music. Not everyone believes that. That's a shame. Part of the problem with the younger musicians is that they don't care about the audience. That's a shame. We're trying to keep jazz alive but it could be more alive. It could be more engaging, it's not as engaging as it could be.

Downloads versus CDs

"Don't let anyone tell you that the CD is dead!" said Gary Walker. Those musicians who insist on presenting their music as digital downloads need to know (maybe they do and don't care) that you can't put metadata into a WAV file. Those files have to be downloaded and burned onto a CD. Someone will have to find the song and title information and find the liner notes (if they exist) to place in the library. That process is time-consuming. On a weekly basis, Derrick Lucas receives twenty to twenty-five physical CDs that range from contemporary to traditional, as well as another twenty to twenty-five downloads to preview. Jazz 90.1 is a twenty-four-hour station with a staff of four paid employees and forty volunteers. They are not an NPR (National Public Radio) affiliate, receive *no* money from the government—it is an all-public, independent station. As a result of a listener survey, they opened up a second stream dedicated to blues with some soul music like Stax in the mix. The average age of listeners during the day is fifty-five to sixty-five; after 9 p.m., the average listener is between twenty-five and thirty-five.

Downloading CDs for radio is a hot topic as we all work to navigate changing platforms. In response to the Facebook post of a frustrated rep, Josh Jackson, Program Director and Content Manager at WVTF Music and Radio IQ, gave a lengthy response detailing some of the issues:

Let's broaden the discussion and talk about the creation and integration of universal metadata standards for jazz and improvised music. Most broadcast organizations use content management systems (ENCO, Audiovault, iMedia, Wide Orbit) for all their audio assets—announcer breaks, promos, liners, and yes . . . music libraries. Many of those are connected to a music database like MusicMasters or something similar. And yes, some stations still use CDs and a live host. There are many underlying factors—management making funding priorities with limited resources, recalcitrance/obstinance, host/user demographics, convenience, or all of the above. Personally, I don't ask for CDs anymore, though I appreciate having physical copies of recordings I like. Most good programmers want to be able to deliver context—not just to forward promote or back-announce a piece of music. Having that information on a press release or some other format does not make an easy workflow. All Information (audio, text, photo) needs to be presented in a way that the announcer can pull salient bits of that information to inform/educate/entertain the audience or to make connections that are not obvious to everyone. Make no mistake—this is all about the audience at the end of this process. Also, sometimes programmers want to be thematic in their choices—songs about "spring" being a very simplistic example ("It Might As Well Be Spring," "Joy Spring," "Spring Can Really Hang You Up the Most," "Spring" by Tony Williams, you get the point). These objectives could all be achieved with a better user interface for the programmer (whether that programmer is a "tastemaker" at a broadcasting outlet or a consumer self-directing their listening on a streaming platform) using a Boolean search function within that. There are lots of organizations who have digitized and many who have not, and even those that have digitized have done it in a haphazard way. THERE IS NO STANDARD. Even those stations who have digitized cannot make a full-time music director become a data entry clerk and fix messy metadata or reconfigure it for data sets specific to their content management systems. I'll stop here for now, but you have to fix the root issue in the marketplace before you can get a nonprofit radio station to come up with a singular solution. I know Apple has made great strides in this aspect of metadata conformity, but again, this needs to be a universally adopted practice—labels, distribution platforms, artists, broadcasters, etc. That's bigger than jazz or radio, but it affects both and all.

Internet Radio

Internet/streaming radio has a more relaxed format. They don't have the same constraints put on them from regulatory agencies imposed on radio stations. Tessil Collins says, "Most musicians can't get their music played on terrestrial radio. I can give people ten spins in a twenty-four-hour cycle that they can't [get] on terrestrial radio that might give you ten spins a week." Yes, Jazz 24/7 is a digital platform, but Tessil still needs a physical CD to input into the system. It is native, not terrestrial, radio and not embraced by a segment of the industry as radio. Those who create digital content only are missing an opportunity for their music to be heard. Tessil explains, "Musicians say to me, 'Guess you won't listen to my CD if you won't download it.' I reply, 'I guess not!' I told one record guy that I don't have time to convert it to listen to find one song to play."

WGBH announcer Eric Jackson downloads and burns to a CD that he'll take to WGBH to play on the air. Tessil says, "That's going backward. It's not a circle, we're on a lineal track. You still want the CD quality of the sound. What's happening is we've gone from vinyl—high-fidelity stereo, to the CD—compressing it down from electronic signals to 0s and 1s. We had to lose a bit of something. Now take that CD to condense to a WAV or MP3 file. If you're listening to a bud speaker in your ear, you won't hear the difference than through a speaker."

A PUBLICIST

Have you wondered why some musicians get more press than others? Or why you are not getting media attention? You have an impressive online presence and get lots of radio airplay but receive little or no mention in print media. At that point, it's time to consider hiring a publicist. Publicity falls under the marketing umbrella and is costly, which is why some labels choose to eliminate that expense from the budget because its results are least quantifiable. Publicists spend their time pitching artists to various media outlets, but their efforts may not bear fruit. Tia Fuller chose to hire a publicist to coordinate her media campaign when she was nominated for a Grammy Award. Her record label, Mack Avenue, has a publicist, but Tia needed more help than they could provide.

I caught up with global award-winning media strategist and consultant Gwendolyn Quinn, who handled Tia's campaign. Her career has spanned more than twenty-five years in communications, entertainment, and media and has paired her with some of the industry's brightest stars, including Aretha Franklin, Whitney Houston, Chaka Khan, Prince, Queen Latifah, and Sean "P. Diddy" Combs, among countless others. "Tia was fun to work with, she has the tolerance level, she's smart, knows how to take control of interviews and has a story to tell. . . . Some artists don't want to do the work and don't care about press." Further, Gwen explains, "When you hire a publicist, you may not get publicity. Expectations—if an artist doesn't understand that [how to be realistic], I won't work with them." Also, know that the artist/publicist relationship is close—they are pushing your brand, all elements must work together. "They're [publicists] there at beginning and end. Closer to an artist than most. Sometimes I will deal with the manager (if they have one) with complaints about the artist. It can be tough to talk to artists directly (if no buffer). I have to be honest with talent even about sensitive things," said Gwen, who likes to work with emerging artists.

If you can afford one at the early stages of your career, having had a publicist will help your branding going forward. One benefit of getting a publicist in the beginning, when you record your first album, is name recognition. Gwen continues, "If you are talented and not sure why no one knows you by your third record, you missed out. Build an audience at the outset. If you're older and frustrated that no one knows you, you may come across as bitter." Also, the delay may have an impact on your future income. We talked about very talented actors who shunned publicity at the outset of their careers to focus on their art. They had respectable careers, got steady work in the theater, and watched their peers skyrocket to Hollywood fame and command huge fees. Which leads back to having a clear vision: do you want fame *and* fortune—or fame *or* fortune?

Think local! Gwen laments, "In this current climate of media hype, artists make the mistake of setting their sights to national attention, only. Artists get confused about the bigger picture and have to do local TV and radio." Also, some media outlets have built-in biases toward artists in some genres. For example, she notes, "Gospel is the hardest genre for publicity . . ." Whereas the *New York Times* and NPR may feature a jazz artist, they will shy away from gospel projects. An industry person confessed to Gwen executives "don't want to hear about Jesus, Lord, and Christ!" Kirk Franklin, CeCe Winans, and Yolanda Adams have been able to break through, but they are exceptions, not the rule.

NOTES

- Have an online presence: be discerning with your social media.
- Always present yourself in a professional manner.
- Get to know industry people.
- Know when to promote yourself and when *not* to promote yourself.

CHAPTER 15

Getting a Job and Keeping It

No matter where you are in your career, when looking for work you have to determine the type of work you seek and if that gig will help you further your business, be compatible with your vision. There is no formula to getting work; not all gigs are equal. Think of yourself as a small business owner with *you* and *your* music as the product. In today's economy, you have to be an entrepreneur. Like any business, you have to build relationships and give people a reason to *buy* your product—to support you. Explore potential revenue streams. Do you want the "bread and butter" gigs like corporate parties, wedding bands, teaching, Broadway shows? Perhaps you want to focus on the low-paying steady gigs or high-visibility festivals. Patience Higgins, "Count Gigula," saxophonist, flautist, multireedist, is one of the hardest-working men in jazz; he does it all. Not only is he an excellent musician, he is the consummate professional with a pleasant demeanor; he is easy to get along with, dependable, on time, dresses appropriately, and is ready to do the job. When I was the administrator for the Jazzmobile Saturday jazz workshop, Patience was one of the instructors and the only teacher whom I had to remind to cash the checks!

Every time you get in front of an audience, you are auditioning for the next job or gig. Your reputation is your calling card. You must present yourself in a professional manner, be presentable, know how to approach people, be amenable, follow up on leads, be assertive, show that you want to work, and have a clear idea of what you want to do. Jeff Clayton put it simply: "Be prepared; be cheerful; as a sideman, don't have an opinion; dress appropriately. Believe me, if they want you, they will call you!"

BUILD RELATIONSHIPS

In the era of "networking," three misused words exchanged at social functions were "Let's do lunch," as they implied dismissal of sorts and a lack of sincerity from the person making the statement, because people didn't follow up. Years ago, I met a young lady in the dressing room at Dizzy's. Shay Stevens indicated that she was interested in doing work in the jazz community but not sure in what capacity. I asked her to reach out to me to further discuss. Months later, she sent me a follow-up email at a time when I was considering finding an assistant. Not only did I hire her, we became good friends. Her jobs with me led her to more work that resulted in her ultimate career change.

Show some class! Relationships are crucial in this business. As long as I've been in this business, there's been an unspoken rule against backstabbing for gigs. There is a protocol. When you are new to the scene, pay attention to the hierarchy, show respect. It's not cool to perform with an artist, then solicit a gig for yourself. It's not cool to befriend someone on social media, then comb through their contacts to "friend" their friends. And, musicians, it's not OK for you to hire someone for the sole purpose of gaining access to their list. On Facebook, guitarist JC Stylles posted about this subject. I found some of the responses alarming.

> **JC Stylles:** People who book you . . . with the ultimate aim to raid your contact list for the names you work with that they don't, or hit up your bandmates on the break right in front of you, or hit up the booker on your gig right in front of you, I'm not sure how to classify these people . . . ???

Commenter A: There are ways to do it and ways not to [. . .]. People say "how can I get that gig?" I think to myself how I've developed a relationship with a venue owner over the course of ten or fifteen years and then someone wants a "gig." I don't blame cats at all BUT I do blame them when they cop an attitude when you simply tell them "this place isn't like that." Anyways, respect.

Commenter B: People that didn't get the memo from Monk "don't sound someone for a gig. Just be on the scene."

Commenter A: If people are looking for "gigs" instead of forming relationships they've already missed the boat.

Commenter C: Yep . . . it's pretty ugly. Artists/musicians who befriend you for the singular purpose of gaining your trust so they can "oh so casually" milk you for all your contacts are equally irksome. It's not new. Started happening to me way back in 1988 when I arrived in NYC. Even so, once you realize it's happening it feels like such a betrayal of trust. Then there are the supposedly "good friend colleagues" who form collaborative relationships with other artists and then give those collaborators your email address who then proceed to solicit you incessantly. Not really very nice. AND last but not least people you realize have gone thru your "friends list" and added everyone they think might boost their "nobody" status to "somebody" or "anybody." This was done by a "singer" who lived in another country to me at the time who was clearly on a mission to elevate her status or FB visibility. I noticed comments appearing on the posts of my colleagues in NYC who I knew she didn't know from a bar of soap. She's still doing it. Sometimes you just have to laugh at the gall of people. They are shameless.

The bottom line is . . . don't be so *damn lazy!* Connect with people, directly. Show up to their gigs, monitor one of their classes. A simple email with "It was great to meet you," "I enjoyed talking to you . . ." goes a long way. Don't get discouraged if the person doesn't immediately respond. I called Ron Carter for two years before he called me back. I've learned much about building relationships from Javon Jackson, who makes five business calls each day. After college, Camille Thurman moved back home and got in touch with people whom she had met while a student; Tia Fuller was one of them. She opened doors for Camille by introducing her to Mimi Jones. "I hooked up with all the women including Antoinette Montague and connected to other musicians (Bill Saxton, Abraham Burton . . .) and studied with them. That led to me getting work as a sub in Charli Persip and Valery Ponomarev's bands." Camille understood how important it is to "create relationships" with people in the industry. She said, "Do your homework, know 'who's who.'" It's not enough to only sound good, she continues, "you have to set yourself apart, don't just show up, there's lots of competition."

HUSTLE

This is your life; work to make things happen. On September 9, 2001, Tia Fuller's dad drove her to New York City from Connecticut after the family's gig. Two days later, the World Trade Center was attacked. "I thought it was an omen," she says. Instead of returning to Denver, she stayed with Javon Jackson (who was also from Colorado and had been a mentor). "It was good to connect with family and I decided all would be well." During her second week, she landed a gig with Tony Williams, an alto player in Cherry Hill, New Jersey. More gigs followed: "I started working at a Def Comedy Jam poetry night (making $75.00 each week), then worked at a church in Jersey City. Then a permanent sub in a private Catholic high school (the kids were a horror), taught for about one year for a half day from 11 to 3 (which allowed me to hang out at night). I taught typing, remedial reading, and something else. Brad Leali and Javon were big helps. Brad, also from Colorado, was in Duke Ellington Orchestra working at Birdland, called me to sub for him (I could double and read), then Jon Faddis as I was booking gigs for my band that led to Sweet Rhythm, my main gig . . ."

No stranger to hustling, Etienne Charles learned early, while a college student. He worked as a sideman in a group that played (for tips) the first Saturday in a restaurant. It turned into a regular gig, and when the leader left, it became his gig. Etienne "learned the ropes and how to be a manager, too." Eventually, he sought out other gigs and got people to come out every night. He moved to New York City to attend Juilliard and landed a record date with percussionist Ralph McDonald in August 2006. At the urging of drummer, Buddy Williams (a staple on Broadway), he joined the union, Local 802. As a result, he got a call to get on the sub list for the play *The Color Purple*. During his tenure at Juilliard, he was "subbing on Broadway." Etienne's advice is "You need to be available and get places quickly."

Be Creative

Think outside the box. Look to have varied income streams. Camille Thurman faced many challenges when she started out. She said, "As a woman, [I saw that] they were creating their own projects even as sidemen. Young people now have fewer work opportunities. Money has to comes from multiple areas now. Teaching, subbing, etc. I like to write. I got work creating my own projects . . . for women it's a necessity." Camille did research to see if her music fit the venue. She took time to put together what she wanted to present. "You have to keep introducing yourself, document all that you do, on film, do a website for people to be able to find you. Be on top of things."

In Chapter 7, you read that Mika Karlsson was able to get work as a result of his sending music clips to his friends that got the attention of a friend who was in charge of music for video games. Before Mika was able to bid for the job, he had to assemble a team. He called some like-minded musicians and formed a company called "Pleasemusicworks." This is what transpired:

> The first thing we did was the video game, I had just come out of school. We produced a demo so we could be sold to

the team. (Electronic Arts has thousands of composers.) You're not hired only as a composer for any big production, but also as a project manager. You have to know all the steps. They give you a large sum of money. They want the files, not the score or performance. (Applied music is something that supports something else.) That's the first hurdle with composers (40 percent of work is composing). They have to know that you won't be late, that you won't f**k up, there is no one to help you, or be delayed, and that it's going to sound great, not just good, and you have a network of people. Tobias knew how to do everything. I knew how to write some tunes. He got the percussionist and the string contractor, got them to do it for free on the threat of not getting called for future work. All of the musicians, [he] got them to make the demo for free (we had no money). We had a thirty-five-piece string orchestra that rehearsed for five hours (we borrowed the studio), then we recorded the demo. My friend at EA said, "Great, I can use this to sell you guys." He sent it to his team; they liked it. Eventually we got the job. (From start to finish took one year. I plant seeds, and one will grow into something. Just keep doing it.)

We were given a big budget to produce it. We hired seventy-five musicians to form a new orchestra, they came from all of the orchestras, we had them for five hours and spent about $35,000. (The whole budget was about 80K, and we spent it all.) It's music for hire because we don't get royalties. Eventually our company failed, we did everything wrong, and we used that game music as our calling card. We didn't know how to run a company. We could have made the soundtrack (forty-five minutes of music) for $35K and pocketed the rest but decided to put a sheen on it because we'd never have that chance again; it was a business card for us. We used the best people and spent the time to make the music sound incredible. It took a long time, and we made many mistakes. Also, we had to pay taxes from that money, so we got a great product. Musicians think we got rich from that, but we didn't, and we showed them that we could do it. What people fear the most in any stage music business, ballet, opera is that people won't deliver either the music or the rest. They just want to call you up. Don't bother them with the details, just deliver. This job prepared me for future projects. I had learned how to mix, how to master, how to boost things using computer sounds, what a team looked like, how musicians should be paid, union scales, contracts, deadlines, and how to talk to a client so they'd understand what you were saying. My advice: know how to do all of the stuff that isn't writing music. You also need a voice. There are millions of people who can write a soundtrack, there are millions of people who can sound like other composers, why should they pick you? My selling point was my classical music because it was a little strange. I'm not coming from the LA soundtrack world of big trailers, I had a flute piece here, I was a bit avant-garde. Be specific when you sell yourself. Be prepared, be specific, know how to hustle.

KNOW WHAT THE JOB REQUIRES

Don't be so eager to take work that you take a job without understanding what the job is. Eric Reed said, "One has to know how to play the gig and know what it requires. I start to think outside the box. I have to look at my scope of skills." That's good advice. Check with the presenter before you plan your show to ensure that your presentation is compatible with the audience. I hired an "upstart" for an outdoor festival who floored me. I'd seen him perform several times in other groups but had not seen him lead his own group. The audience was diverse in terms of age and race, so I expected him to play a set of standards; instead, he chose to perform his original (race-conscious) music that wasn't compatible with the crowd. What surprised me was his awareness, beforehand, that might not have been the right setting for his music. The fact that he questioned himself yet performed anyway gave me pause. His performance was reminiscent of the hilarious *Saturday Night Live* skit featuring Eddie Murphy as a reggae artist, hired for a reception, and singing: "kill da white people," as the audience looked aghast. When he finished, the host said, "I thought that he was going to sing 'Day O.'"

What *Not* to Do

Don't take the gig if you're not into it! I hired a guy whom I had to chase down to get his contract. I also got him an interview on WBGO a few days before the gig. He had to drive in from somewhere to get there. (He said to me: "I didn't know that the interview was part of the gig." It wasn't, but rather a courtesy that WBGO extended to us.) At the interview, the announcer asked, "What time is the gig?" The musician said: "I don't know, I was going to ask you." This, mind you, was *on air*. Needless to say, I was pissed. Know how long the set is before you show up. Don't ask "How long is the gig?" right before you're about to go up onstage. And don't ask how long the break is—especially when there is no break. (Look at the contract, or ask the manager before the gig.) Don't cut the set short.

Don't Do a Bait and Switch

For the last few years, a musician has been calling me to book his band. He lives in California, and the festivals are in New Jersey. Many years ago, his group had performed at Jazz in the Garden, and I was interested in having him back. I finally agreed to give him a date. Though he usually works with a large ensemble, he was willing to bring a smaller group that would fit our small budget. To my surprise, he asked me to provide some of the backline that he needed, and he wanted us to pay for a hotel room. I had been clear with him at the outset that we did not have it in our budget to rent any equipment or money for the hotel. He reluctantly agreed to using our backline, then told me that he would not be able to give us the type of performance that would highlight his skills. During our conversation, I agreed that our venue was not a good fit for him, so I canceled the gig.

Also, it's not good to sign a contract and then try to renegotiate, demanding more things. Or hijack the contract to hold as bait for more money. Early on in my booking career, a musician did that to me. He would not return my calls, so I showed up at his gig to confront him. Outside the club, he told me that, for more money, he'd bring a larger group than agreed upon. Had the brochure not been printed, I'd have fired him. I was able to give him the money that he asked, but I've never hired him again.

Be On Time

I cannot emphasize this enough! Be on time for sound checks. Some bands work so much that they don't have to do them, but as the leader, it behooves you to go to the venue early if it's new to you. It's to make sure everything is to your satisfaction. You need to give yourself time for things to go wrong (they will). Some leaders have a reputation for arriving moments before a performance. Others have sidemen who are notoriously late. Two incidents stand out. I hired a musician notorious for his tardiness. Knowing his reputation, I threatened his manager that I wouldn't pay him if he was late. Thankfully he did show up, on time, for sound check (I was nervous). However, his drummer came running in about five minutes before show time. We provided the drum kit so he only had to bring his cymbals. Still, it was a close call.

Another musician I hired on the heels of his meteoric rise was early because I'd driven him to the museum after picking him up at WBGO, where I'd arranged an interview. In the contract I stipulated that we open the gate at 11:45 a.m. Sound check is between 10:30 and 11:30 a.m. Some groups don't need the entire hour, but they'll tell me beforehand if that's the case. Everyone in the band was late. The bass player arrived right before we let in the crowd. Imagine my horror when I saw the bassist pluck a string, then the neck broke from the bottom, rendering it useless. He and the leader were trying to put it back together, but like Humpty Dumpty, they couldn't. I called every bass player I knew in and around Newark, before finding one who (he plays electric, not upright) lived in South Orange, New Jersey. I'd sent some guys to pick it up. While they were en route, a gentleman sitting in the front row said that he had a bass at home and went to get it. The first thirty minutes, the leader was bassless. After the concert, I chided him for not reining in his sideman; his reply, "It didn't matter, the bass would have broken anyway." To him, I said, "Yes, but had it happened earlier, I would have had more time to find a solution."

YOUR APPROACH

Learn how to communicate. You need to know how to talk to people. As a curator, I am dumbfounded at the lack of professionalism I encounter. Growing up, I was taught to respect my elders and could not call them by their first names unless given permission by them. It was made clear to me, as a child, that I was not on equal footing with adults and that I was to address them with respect regardless of who they were. Which brings me to this chapter. I find the current scene troubling. Young people need to understand hierarchy and learn how to talk with elders. Recently, I introduced a young musician to an elder of mine. Instead of saying, "It's nice to meet you," he said, "So what are *you* into?" I was amazed at his familiarity with a stranger. This is not an indictment of all young people. In the first edition of this book, Eric Reed cited Ulysses Owens as an example of someone who he saw to have promise and why: "I still get excited listening to extremely talented young musicians. I recently worked with a drummer—Ulysses Owens—in his twenties, who has given me great hope and great expectations. He is a beautiful person, has a beautiful attitude, he's a consummate professional, and he plays his ass off. Those types of musicians are so rare. Some musicians have horrible attitudes and act as though they are doing you a favor by playing with *you!*"

Veteran musicians, who should know better, need to learn some etiquette, as well. Familiarity is no excuse for a lack of professionalism. There is a fine line between bullying and being assertive. This is a short list of what musicians have said or asked me when trying to get a gig. None of these approaches are effective:

"Hey, when you gonna give me a gig?"

"I want to do _____."

"My artist wants to do your festival, give me a date."

"How come you won't hire me for _____?"

"What do I have to do to get you to hire me?"

"Are you gonna have me on Jazz in the Garden this summer?"

Instead, how about some of these approaches? These would be far more likely to result in future gigs:

"I hope that you will consider my band for . . ."

"I love your lineup for _____. I'm working on _____, which might be a good fit for . . ."

"Thank you for hiring me in the past. Please consider me again, as I have a new band or project that your audience may enjoy."

BE ASSERTIVE

If you believe that you have something to offer, speak up. Let people know what you are working on. Don't take "no" for an answer. Every few months, or year, ask again. Some situations call for you to be assertive, just as Michael Wolff was with Cal Tjader. The day he got fired at Fantasy, Michael was walking around the halls when he spotted Cal:

I was walking around Fantasy Records, and I saw Cal, whom I recognized. I said, "Let me introduce myself," and I said, "I'm Michael Wolff, and I'm ready to play in your band." (I was cocky; I was eighteen or nineteen), and he said, "Well, I'll be playing at El Matador in San Francisco [which was considered *the* jazz club]; come sit in." So, I went and sat in, and it worked out. So that's how I got the gig.

However, not all persistence pays off. You should be able to intuit when to leave people alone. James Browne says,

> I have given gigs to musicians who have been consistently assertive, but there are others who can call me forever, and I won't hire them. I choose what I want to sell. You can't go to Barney's and ask them why they won't sell cornflakes. I have said to musicians that there is nothing that says, "equal opportunity"; this is a business. I've never gone to a musician and asked, why don't you have such-and-such in your band? They would not take kindly to that.

SUPPORT THE SCENE

Bobby Sanabria told a funny story about trying to get a gig at a club: "Max Roach saw me at a jazz club once. He was listening to the music as I was trying to get a gig at the club, and Max said to me, 'If I was in your situation, it would behoove me to patronize the establishment and buy a drink.' That was a lesson." Mika Karlsson concurs: "*Show up* to all the premieres of the houses. Support your peers! Even if it costs more than you can afford. Don't always ask to be on the list. Ask when you don't need!" More on this topic in Chapter 16.

BE VERSATILE

The stigma of crossing genres is gone. Drummer Victor Lewis had worked with Dexter Gordon *and* David Sanborn at the same time. He told me that he had to adapt his sound to each situation because he didn't want the jazz guys to know that it was *he* who was working with Sanborn and vice versa, he didn't want to get labeled as a sellout. Musicians have always crossed genres, that's not new. Now the industry is more accepting of musicians who do.

Mika Karlsson addressed the challenges he faces as a composer: "There are no homes for composers anymore. You have to be a salesman. There are no record labels to take care of you, though in classical there never was except for the big names. You can't sell scores to make a living, can't wait for commissions. Now classical is a hybrid kind of business. In a way it's easier now to work." He was looked down on as a classical composer because he was doing commercial work. "Things have changed now and that is accepted. Composers want to have fun, and classical composers have bands now."

Dorothy Lawson and Paula Kimper, too, have taken risks. I asked Dorothy what musical demands were placed on her to play with Ron Carter, and if she had to change *how* she played. She replied, "*No*, I don't have to change anything he writes, with such an empathy for the full cello sound, I think that is what he wants. Phrasing inside his music is more rhythmically propelled than a lot of classical music is. I feel tempted and provoked to explore different ways of accenting the rhythms and jazzy melodies than if I was playing classical music."

NOTES

- Reach out to mentors.
- Check out the scene.
- Don't always have your hand out; offer to help (be in service to others).
- Follow up.

CHAPTER 16

The Art of "The Hang"

To "hang" (verb) has several meanings. To stay and to spend time relaxing in a place or with a friend can take on the pejorative that one is wasting time. For the purpose of this chapter, "the hang" is what one does to be on the scene, to get recognized, to make connections, to learn.

My moniker "Queen of Hang" was given to me by a fellow announcer, Michael Bourne. In 1995, I was hired to host *Sunday Morning Harmony* on WBGO, Newark, 88.3FM. My knowledge of the music did not match that of my colleagues, and I felt that I needed to get up to speed as fast as possible. WBGO is one of the premier jazz radio stations in the country, and I didn't want to be a weak link. Before hosting the show, I had also gone through training to host a TV show on Manhattan Neighborhood Network (MNN). I thought that the best way to learn about the music was from the musicians, but my boss would not allow interviews on that show. As a result, I decided that I would do a show on MNN and call it *The Art of Jazz*. My problem was that I didn't know many musicians, so I decided to go meet them. I put myself on a weekly schedule to check out clubs, go to jam sessions, etc. I'd get off work from my day job, then hit the clubs. I hung with a purpose; the scene became my classroom. At the risk of sounding nostalgic, when I started out in radio (1995), the scene was different. From then to around 2006, I'd see older guys show up for younger musicians and vice versa. Over the years I'm struck at how little I see this happening. As of this writing, I went to see Will Calhoun with Kevin Eubanks, Marcus Strickland, and Christian McBride perform at the premier Blue Note club in New York City. Roy Haynes and Bernard "Pretty" Purdie were there, but I didn't see younger musicians. Bobby Sanabria confirmed that there is a disconnect between generations and that students are telling *him* to check *them* out. From hanging out and meeting and seeing so many musicians I spun on the radio when I started curating, I had seen enough performances to know who was good. I miss some of the clubs that are closed, like Cecil's Jazz Club in New Jersey and Sweet Rhythm because I met so many people I might not have met otherwise with whom I now have personal connections. I made it my business to get to know industry people. That's what the hang is about.

The hang is a way for you, regardless of genre, to connect with people in your industry. Mika talked about the importance of using nonwork time with your colleagues: "Spend enough time with these people without needing something back. That is when they discuss things [like projects they are working on], when they're socializing. Then stay in touch, something *may* come of it . . ." Will Calhoun agrees:

> The hang is important—you gotta keep a barometer on it. When we were growing up in the street (not the industry but hip-hop), we had to know when to go, when "to bounce." If after three events nothing was happening, we went home, because we knew, at that point, something not good was gonna happen. Pay attention to the room, the energy of hanging. Don't hang just to hang. Have goals, follow them, have a flow chart, write it on a piece of paper, not on your phone, something you can look at like a bird or a tree. Know what a week means, what an hour means,

planning for two weeks, how are you preparing for that? I'm trying to get to there and this hanging really isn't helping me out.

The reality is that, as Camille Thurman stated, "to hang with mentors is gold. You learn how to handle business, how to speak to people." Tia Fuller shares her perspective. She states, "The Hang—two tiers: social and bonding with your peers, sitting in with folks; they become family. That's getting more lost. Social media is having a negative impact on it. Folks don't know how to speak to elders, get the information and show reverence. This is not happening as much as in the past. [Young people] are not on the same level as elders; that includes schools. To be on a first-name basis is cool, but don't get confused, you're not on the same level because it's a casual environment. Mentoring is part of it [the hang] too."

Not all hanging is the same. For example, neither Jeremy Pelt nor Ulysses Owens "hung."

Ulysses suggests that the definition of the hang needs to be clarified. Some people are so busy hanging it elicits a "birds of a feather flock together" mentality. You should "hang with people on your level or above. . . . There are different types of hang. I never went to jam sessions but I pursued people who had what I needed. I targeted people to be mentors . . ." When he connected with Mulgrew Miller, he asked him about music that he needed to listen to. He continues, "Figure out what the person's interest is, send thank-you notes, and always look to the next generation." Jeremy chose to create a "scene" at an understated club instead of the usual haunts.

So much that happens in the music business is because of personal contact. Countless times I have observed musicians ignore people until they find out who they are. Don't think that this goes unnoticed, and it might be held against you down the line. It took Allan Harris some time to realize what he needed to do to be in New York. By his own admission, he was not well received when he first arrived: "I didn't go out and go to things like IAJE [International Association of Jazz Educators]; I did not network enough. *Duh . . . This is New York*

City, and you have to present yourself, like hanging out, interviews, promoting. I had no concept of that, and I had a clown manager." No matter what level you are at, you must be visible.

Jeremy Pelt shares some advice:

> This is a people-based business. You have to be outgoing but not annoying. Establish relationships. Be realistic. Have something to offer. Have something to speak about. Establish yourself with a club owner. Be on the scene. I appointed some as mentors. I'm always in contact with and looked up to Eddie Henderson. I had made myself available to Freddie Hubbard. I looked at careers of who I wanted to model myself after; (the late) Roy Hargrove was one of them. Roy, he had respect of his elders (my Aunt June loved Roy, too). I didn't go to the hot spots, I went to Cleopatra's Needle (and created a scene), and Wynton Marsalis and Roy would come by . . .

Think of the hang as a classroom without being in school. There you learn the nuances of the business beyond your instrument. According to Etienne Charles:

> The hang is crucial because to me the hang, if you're religious, you have church then after church then before church. Then there's the part after the service where people are mingling, there might be food but that's important—a support system for the congregation. When I think about the hang, it makes me think what people told me about Bradley's and Augie's. It's a way for you to interact with people you want to be like. Also, people you want to be around. The hang is a way to network and for you to learn beyond your instrument. To hear Dizzy tell a story, or Jimmy Heath (if a piano was around he'd go to the piano and show you harmony). If they're around

they'll bless us with something. After Christian McBride's fortieth birthday, a Monday night at Dizzy's, the place had closed down. Ulysses and I rapped with him, then he and I went downtown and ran into Robert Glasper, then about six other hip cats. . . . Knowledge is being poured into you when you hang. They may even suggest a book for you to read. It's a way to feel reassured when you are around people like them. They pick you up and put you on their shoulders. . . . I'm older now and pass down things I've learned from, say, Joe Wilder. Also, now I give cats industry advice. You learn how to dress, how to act. You meet people who might call you for a gig. Back in the day if you didn't hang, no one would call you because folks didn't have phones. Johnny Mandel told me about a spot where musicians would hang and wait for calls. You learn the history when talking to older cats.

Etienne reminded me that he and I met in 2006 at the Lenox Lounge and that I was there with Eric Reed and Kahlil Kwame Bell. He also recalled, "It was Monty Alexander's gig with Herlin Riley on drums and Reginald Veal on bass." Talk about great recall!

Aaron Diehl, who is almost an elder statesman (at the age of thirty-three), hangs less because he's on the road so often. But when he is in New York City, he does go hear music, though that's "not the same as 'hang,' which is social." He now uses his time wisely "to hear the musicians, like late night at Dizzy's. I want to get to know young musicians and hear what they're into. I used to hang at Small's then go eat . . . great days. . . . If in New York City, it's a rite of passage."

NOTES

- Learn how to hang.
- Be gracious.
- Don't be angry.
- Seek out mentors.
- Make yourself an asset to your community outside of musicianship.
- Support the venues where you may want to work.
- Follow mentors, reach out the them, meet them where they are. Find something in common with them.

CHAPTER 17

Your Money: Contracts, Royalties, and Streaming

Music is a business. It's about commerce: do people want to buy what you are selling—*you*?

Learn how to price yourself; know your value; remember, if they called you, they want you. Fees vary across genres. I know of musicians who command higher fees in jazz when hired in another genre (e.g., gospel) but are paid a fraction of what their counterparts might make. Pop and contemporary artists generally command higher wages than most, but their money might greatly fluctuate as their popularity ebbs and flows. I know of one artist who went from $35,000 to $250,000 then down to $125,000 per show in a six-year span.

Should you land a gig with an orchestra, you will be paid a salary. Dorothy Lawson of ETHEL explains that the organization "has chosen to pay its members a monthly retainer, like a salary. All activities are included. Some months are very heavy, others are completely free. The workload amortizes itself, and we appreciate the consistency of the payments."

KNOW YOUR VALUE

Can you sell out large halls with patrons who will pay anywhere from $35 per ticket to $200 and up? Jeff Clayton explained:

There is no one set way or set formula to figure out your fee, but there are components that work better for one area but not others. You have to manipulate the numbers to fit your situation . . . let's say the hall seats one hundred people, you have a five-piece band, and you want to make $1,000. Find out how much money per seat that the $1,000 represents. You take into account the size of the room (the number of seats), the price per seat, subtract two-thirds, the approximate cost of the hall rental, and other expenses, and the money that is left is the profit that is available for you as a band. If they have sponsors, then your fee will not be based on ticket sales alone, but on how much the sponsors have contributed. If the sponsors are well-known companies, most likely the venue will have more money to offer. If the fee offered to you is not acceptable, you can factor in your stature: Have you performed there before? Do you have a new CD to sell? You have to look at all those things. Also, look at the standard amount of money that others have been paid for that same event. Keep your ear to the ground—talk to other musicians to find out what they have been paid. When I'm told that other musicians on my level will accept a fee that I won't accept, then I get an idea how much others get paid.

If you are not comfortable saying that you don't want to play a particular gig, one way to get out of it is to set your fee above what you know the person will pay. Says Jeff Clayton, "I price myself *out* of a gig if I don't want to do it." But beware—the presenter might surprise you by paying your high fee, so it might be best to just say that you are booked that day.

Make the numbers work for you. My foray into producing was at the Newark Museum. They had a large budget for Black History Month programming and a small one for Jazz in the Garden. I was able to pay a group for Black History Month about three times what I paid for a group for JIG. That summer, I hired a guy who'd been in one of the BHM bands. Not knowing how much he'd been paid for that gig, it was not until he arrived at the museum with the man who'd been the leader that I found out that what I offered him for a group was what he'd been paid by the leader in February. We had not discussed how many musicians he was bringing, but I did expect, at least, a trio. Admittedly, what I was paying him was low; he made the money work for him, I understood!

In situations where fees are set, like union gigs, you still have room to negotiate, though it may not be money. Mark Gross says, "You are worth as much as you can get! Yes, you can throw out a price but you can also negotiate for promotional things. [If you're on Broadway,] you might ask to be listed in the *Playbill* or used in their advertising . . . they called you, they want you."

Last year, Mika released seven albums (opera and dance). He now stipulates in all of his contracts that every performance must be recorded: "If I can't get enough money to record it, I ask them to have it recorded (always document your work) so that it has a life beyond the show itself; the show may be a flop. That's the luxury of being in dance, I get a lot of rehearsals with the ensemble or orchestra and get a lot of performances (from them) and I've been able to sell it as an extra perk to the audience that it's available on Spotify the night of the premiere. That's something the opera house had never thought about. [I tell them], 'How nice would it be [if] when you walk out the night of the premiere you can listen to the music on Spotify? You're not gonna make money selling it; no one will buy the CD in the gift shop.' Be a progressive opera house that does this for your audience and make it a better experience for them coming."

CONTRACTS

Bassist Ray Brown told pianist James Williams, "Always read the fine print; it is never good news." Artists *and* presenters have to protect themselves from harm. Early on in my curatorial capacity, I learned how to read a contract. One October, I was approached by someone who expressed interest in performing the following February for our

Black History Month Program. She was the first artist I'd chosen for BHM, so she got first pick of dates. Very efficiently, she quickly sent me her detailed contract—I looked at it with a glance—with a deposit request (in most cases, contracts were generated by the museum). I processed her deposit payment and proceeded to book the rest of the month. Days before we were to send the newsletter to the printer, she called to tell me that she needed to change her date because she needed to take an exam. What began as a pleasant request escalated into ire when I told her that if the other performers' schedules didn't allow, I'd have to hold her to the date. She didn't back down, I reread her contract to discover that she had protected *herself* against *any* cancellation, meaning she could keep her deposit and the museum was obligated to find a spot for her that year. It worked out that one of the other artists was able to switch dates with her, but that experience taught me a lesson: read contracts and let the artists know what you can and can't do once you've perused it. My boss wasn't happy at the performer's aggression during negotiations and forbade me from hiring her again.

Write down everything you want. Be specific. Eric Reed: "I ask for everything that I want . . . down to the type of water that I want. I ask for salted cashews, water—no Evian—to the number of towels that I want on the stage and the numbers of bottles of water that I want on the stage." What musicians ask for is revealing. They have asked for cognac and honey-baked ham in their dressing rooms. Some are vegans. Others like wine and beer. I find riders fascinating.

Always double-check the details before the gig. Etienne Charles got a valuable lesson the first time he was hired to do late night set at Dizzy's. Todd Barkan, who booked the club, hired him to do the late set during the week that Randy Weston was headlining. It was January 2008. At that point, Dizzy's had three sets on Friday and Saturday nights. The contract had that Etienne would go on at 1:00 a.m. He recalled,

> It was a Friday night and I was home taking a nap. I got a call from Todd, who said, "Where are you?" This was at 11

p.m., and I was in bed taking a nap. Todd said that Randy didn't do three sets (Randy was in his eighties). It would have been nice to know that beforehand! The contract said we'd go on at 1 a.m., so this taught me to go beyond what's in the contract and double-check with [the] promoter to make sure that all the times are solid. I called the guys in the band to get there right away. We had to start with a trio, waiting for the horn player, so we started playing the blues. We ended up playing a two-hour set. That was one of the best gigs of my life . . .

Be Honest

My first month on staff at the museum, I hired Eric Reed to perform in the auditorium using the grand piano. I had had it tuned, so I thought all was well. After his performance, he told me how bad the piano was, and had I not been a friend, he might not have played on it. Because of his honesty, I was able to convince the directors to purchase new pianos. Eric recalled, "Everything is negotiable; you have to be flexible. If the piano is bad . . . you never assume: as Samuel L. Jackson said, if you assume, you make an *ASS* out of *U* and *ME*. Never assume that people know anything. Not everyone knows what you require, especially people you have never worked with." That ended up being a win-win for both Eric and the Newark Museum.

FOLLOW YOUR MONEY

Since the Napster debacle, the record industry has been working to deal with the financial problems associated with Internet downloading and other things. Tessil Collins shed light on the issues surrounding Napster:[1]

---

1   Napster was guilty of contributory and vicarious infringement of the plaintiffs' rights to intellectual property, which were routinely traded by means of Napster's online facilities. It was unceremoniously bought and folded into Rhapsody, a competing music subscription service. But Napster's glory days were its first three years, before it filed for bankruptcy.

We had that period in the nineties—Napster—where everybody was in shit for nothing. And the CD was going out of style at the same time as these files. I could attach a file to your email, you'd get the song. You could go to the renegade website that had all the music on it and go download it. Eventually, they caught up with folks who were doing it, but it changed—I'll be bold—people have now lost the value of paying for music, and [this is] why vinyl is so interesting because people can spend money for more than something that is just some bit on their computer or phone. Artists have to embrace it. Musicians have to see the return of pressing up CDs because they still have to do it for radio, for the radio music industry is still tactile—we get 50 CDs/week. If you think that I'm gonna stop my other work and then go find a digital file and convert it and download in the system . . . I can see the stack of CDs in front of me. I'm not [. . .] going to download everything and not going to pay attention . . . in other words, musicians should think about the user experience.

Digital Sales

To make sure that the artist/composer obtains mechanical royalties, they should belong to one of the performing-rights organizations, such as ASCAP, BMI, or SESAC. In the "old days," pre-Internet, chasing down royalties wasn't easy. Now it is with the International Standard Recording Code (ISRC), a unique international identifier for sound and music video recordings. Unlike the Universal Product Code (UPC), the ISRC is tied to the recording in the track and not the carrier of the track (CD or digital sound file). In short, the ISRC identifies individual tracks, while the UPC identifies the complete album. For singles, you definitely need an ISRC code for the track. It is highly recommended that you also get a UPC code for singles because a UPC code is *required* on a single by:

- iTunes
- Nielsen SoundScan to participate in the Billboard Charts
- Retailers, if you plan to release it as a physical CD

Disk makers and even some of the aggregators, streaming sites, and download sites, like CD Baby, will do it for you. Disk makers offers different packages that include acquiring the codes, or you may want to get them yourself. ISRC codes are primarily used to identify and catalog individual songs (tracks) on an album. The ISRC allows you to get paid for digital music sales by ensuring that your royalties are tracked properly. ISRC codes are necessary to sell your individual tracks via iTunes and other online music distributors. They are also required for any songs that you plan to offer for streaming on Spotify and other streaming services. Jeff Clayton cautioned, "Musicians must make sure that the information attached to those codes is THEIR information, not the disk maker's, because your money (royalties) is directed to whatever is coded on that recording."

Mika is a DIY guy:

> You don't have to go through labels, you can't just call up Apple Music. It costs $50 a year to get any album on all the services. I upload my album and artwork. (I can't be bothered going through labels, nor do I want to give away half the rights to it. No middleman.) I can't wait for a label to do it, and I make all of the royalties and don't want to wait for someone to release my music and I don't want to give away half the rights because I want to make all the royalties. TuneCore takes 20 percent. I usually make enough to keep paying the $50 a year. They pay for themselves. If someone wants to use a track on a film, the label would [usually] take half, [but this way] I get everything.

Ulysses Owens Jr. initially issued his recording *Songs of Freedom* digitally, with an official release date a month later. That allowed him to get Google alerts that it's on some streams. Streaming allows music people to listen without having to buy it. "My album, I get a percentage for every spin (cents); the label calculates it. Different services give different percentages with musicians."

One of the reasons for those paltry percentages is that the rules governing the Internet are different, as opposed to (terrestrial) radio. According to Tessil,

> We (Internet) pay a lot more money to play music, a lot more money; we have to pay for performance, the radio folks don't. Artists' complaints about not getting much money from streaming—it's true! Not because the math is wrong; [it's] the pot of money, relative to the millions of musicians who are out there. . . . Two years ago, people like me—folks just folded up and went away, Live365, Last.fm, they just went away. They had to because they were like a syndicated pipe so all the little guys could go to one place, and people could just cherry-pick this station, that station. Then the government came in, finalized the rules, they realized that they could be financially liable for something they weren't making any money on. It's a catch-22.

"Who's making the money?" I ask. "The agencies BMI, ASCAP, the regulatory people and the government are making the money!"

Royalties

Composers for ballet and opera have multiple income streams available. Mika writes for both. He explains:

> We get a composition fee that can range between a few thousand dollars to $100,000, then you get to negotiate the grand rights (separate from everything), that becomes your royalty schedule. The first run you don't make royalties because they're paying you a composition fee. If popular demand is high and they program it again the next year, they'll pay you royalties (up to your negotiation—you get

a percentage of box office). If it wasn't a good piece, they shouldn't be hit with royalties—so it's an incentive for me to make it good. I get paid a fee if someone else wants to produce it. (I hate negotiating, so I have a lawyer do that.) On a good deal, I'll make between 10 and 13 percent of box office that can amount to more (or less) depending on the initial fee. [If he had a publisher, that's the fee the publisher would have taken half of.] . . . I make money off of my recorded music, if someone licenses it; I make money from TV. Record sales, not so much . . .

Streaming

Pharrell Williams had a spectacular 2014 with his hit song, "Happy," that topped the charts in the United States and two dozen other countries, selling 6.4 million copies and garnering him a Grammy win for Best Pop Solo Performance. It was also in heavy rotation on the digital radio platform Pandora, streaming 43 million times in the first quarter alone, yet Sony/ATV Music Publishing says it received just $2,700 (for songwriting) from Pandora for plays of the tune during that period, which they split with him. For performance rights during that period, he received $25,000. The debate about streaming and royalty payment ensued when Taylor Swift pulled her music from Spotify, telling Yahoo, "I'm not willing to contribute my life's work to an experiment that I don't feel compensates the writers, producers, and creators of this music, and I just don't agree with perpetuating the perception that music has no value and should be free."

Swift is a superstar who can afford to make that choice, but can the average musician? Ulysses Owens says, "*No!*" He contends that "if you are not streaming, no one will know that your CD exists." As a recording artist and producer, he knows all too well the financial downside of streaming but acknowledges its importance:

Streaming is huge! But we need to figure out as artists other reasons why we need to make music. [Given the] fact that streaming is in existence, we are no longer going to make money the way we used to make money from it. We'll only make money from touring, or getting commercially licensed, or figuring out some new way to monetize it. The idea behind streaming strips away the reality that we'll ever make a lot of money selling this music, that idea it is pretty much dead. I think musicians need to figure out why we are making records. Need to figure out new ways records can be applicable in society. We need to be in tune with streaming, the rates and the rules behind it, and all that stuff because we'll never make money the same way.

How Did We Get Here?

To understand streaming, I turned to my friend Tessil Collins, Managing Director of Jazz at WGBH. After spending twenty-seven years working in the Boston public schools as a teacher and administrator, he retired. Upon retirement in January 2013, he started the Internet radio station Sun Music, which streams online 24/7 from Dorchester, Massachusetts. He has been working with digital content from the ground up and can address the issues of these "emerging technologies" that he likens to "a new artist, band and/or musician starting out who no one knows, that you don't have to pay much money to because they don't have value and they don't have to be paid lots of money to get."

He explains:

> Streaming is a vehicle, it's like you're in the water streaming along; you can be in a boat or on a raft or you could be on different things on this stream. You know streaming as radio rebroadcast on the Internet. It's still terrestrial broadcast radio, it's just coming down another pipe. It's not native. What I'm doing on Sun Music and *Jazz 24/7* is native. It's not terrestrial, we're not on an antenna, we're not under FCC rules, and we don't have live people. Now we're dealing with screens and views. Listeners but views [too].
>
> For those of us who are old enough to remember a radio, that box next to your bed or in another area in your

home, it is almost obsolete. People are now listening on a phone, a tablet, and/or on a computer and are now registered as "data." Of the people who listen to *Jazz 24/7*, 60 to 70 percent are listening on a mobile device and are considered data. As much as we put lots of time in the web presence, the page, the player—people ain't sitting at a desktop listening. Where are the artists on this? Again, dating myself, streaming as far as I'm concerned is the 45 record. Remember that?

Growing up, I went to the store (the distributors were in downtown Roxbury) and could go to the warehouse to get a 45 for fifty cents, as opposed to a dollar at the record stores. The single is how the songs got out there, which then made folks go buy the album. That's all gone now.

We're in territory now where lots of our older musicians are still learning how to embrace the difference; the learning curve part is still off. They have to learn to interact with [technology]; you have to use it. I was trying to book some local artists here that would have been good for a show I was working on but they don't use email . . . sixty to seventy years old. [I] needed an answer right away. If you want to be part of the running, you got to keep up. Faxes don't exist, they wanted me to mail the stuff . . . not gonna happen, we need input right away. They complained about "I don't like doing all that stuff." Too bad. It's a lot.

Back to emerging platforms: they are web-based anything, including podcasts. This is Native Internet. There are few people doing it as if they're on a radio station, Internet only. They're on like it's terrestrial radio. This allows people who couldn't do it on the radio before to shift emphasis to that product; it's only a pipe. (People are watching TV over a stream, not watching over the air. We grew up with three channels and needed an antenna; now we have a port in a wall that goes to a cable; it's a signal over the wire. Satellite is a transmission from a satellite to a tower to a wire, so it's more like terrestrial radio. I'm talking about something that originates on the Internet and has different rules.)

Problem: sending WAV files, because those are the files that have more fidelity than MP3 files, but you can't put metadata into a WAV file (information such as album name, artist names, album cover, song titles). If you're gonna use it, who's going to put in that data? We have to put the information in if we're gonna use it. Everything has it, your phone, etc. You have to have the software to convert the file. Most people don't know what to do with them after they download them.

Musicians are screwed in terms of digital delivery, not streaming—how are consumers getting their music? To get it digitally, you go to iTunes, Amazon, to one of these places, and download files from them; they are the stores. There are ships like me who take their music down the stream so people can hear it, as opposed to ships that are taking music up the antenna and blasting it over the air. There are no CDs, so they can't go to Tower Records or Sam Goody's to buy a physical CD. The difference in cost—the single digital file is a dollar, that's what a 45 was, but now we don't have radio stations that are playing singles like that. You'll be listening to a station, and they'll play only select artists because of dayparting; some stuff won't play during the day, but I'll play everything, all day—there's so much music.

NOTES

- Know that you can negotiate contracts.
- Learn to know your value.
- Register all of your music with one of the agencies.
- Make sure that your IRCS codes have the proper information.

CHAPTER 18

Do You Need a Manager? An Agent?

Let's face it, the traditional business model of artist/management/agent/record label has shifted. No longer do you need a machine behind you to succeed, but you should understand the difference between the manager and the agent. At one time, managers' names were synonymous with the artists they managed; Joe Glaser and Louis Armstrong, Colonel Parker and Elvis Presley, John Levy and Nancy Wilson. Managers were instrumental in directing their careers to prominence. The industry was such that artists needed someone who could forge inroads into venues around the world, negotiate record deals—they monitored all aspects of their lives. Artist manager Laura Hartmann explained, "A manager is to help an artist develop his/her career. In an ideal situation, a manager will assemble a team to achieve that. She/he will bring together a lawyer, a record company, a publicist, and a radio person. The manager and artists are partners. They make sure that those parts work effectively together to create opportunities for the artist to see that her/his stars are on the rise."

On the other hand, a booking agent gets you work. According to Laura Hartmann, "As a manager, I cannot legally be a booking agent, I need a license to do that. I get my artists noticed, but I am not a booking agent, I'm a manager. I am looking for a partner who cares as much about my clients as myself, so I can form a booking division. Management and booking should be under one roof and working for the same goal."

As a solo artist, Will Calhoun has been approached by people seeking to manage him. His first question to them is "'Why?' I ask them if they can get me X number of gigs, a certain amount of money for the sidemen, will you get me into certain venues next year? What's *your* plan?" If they can't answer those questions, he knows they have no clue, or skill set, to manage him. He continues, "A manager gets you from point A to point Z (or somewhere in between). It's not what it used to be. I want to hear what their strategy is: what will you do for me?"

Management is different among genres. Will explained, "Pop music taught me the definition of management. Jazz folks aren't necessarily educated. Puff Daddy (a.k.a. P. Diddy or Sean Combs) worked for years, *for free*, behind some ruthless managers. . . . Artists have to educate them[selves] about what they want. Madonna knew what she wanted in 1980, so we weren't surprised with her success. Management? What does that mean to you? I'm already doing it myself. Artists have to be educated about the business and know what they want."

DO YOU *NEED* A MANAGER?

Ron Carter has mixed feelings about the need for managers:

> I think that question deserves a two-pronged answer. Musicians have weaned themselves from being responsible for their musical actions off the bandstand. The result is they need someone to speak on their behalf. What that has done is separate them from the business—and that is not a good thing—and from other musicians. Personal contact is eliminated. I've had dealings with guys who have me call their manager—they don't have their schedules and won't talk to me directly. A manager will take out his share of the money before he pays the musicians. I

abhor that. You think this guy is so irresponsible that you will take your percent before he gets his pay and pays his band? You want a share of his [artist's] publishing company, and you have not written any words to his songs, and you want your part of *his* money? I don't think so! Managers have been allowed to take over more than they have a right to take over, because musicians have abdicated their right to be responsible for things they should be responsible for.

In the early part of Javon Jackson's career, he had management. At that time, having one raised your stature and you could be more aggressive about creating opportunities for yourself. At a point, he asked himself if he was "viable for management." He said, "I didn't feel I was viable enough, meaning I didn't think I was committed enough to my career to the point where I was applicable for management. Sometimes you have to be realist. Management helps you make the right kinds of choices, decisions to put your career on an upward trajectory. . . . At that time I was doing lots of sideman things, I wasn't going all the way to be a leader."

Eric Reed understands the fluidity of management. The stage of one's career will determine what you need:

> By and large, most managers function as high-priced assistants. The average musician doesn't need a manager or a booking agent, but the average musician, with eyes to be a leader, needs a personal assistant. You need a buffer, a mouthpiece to intercept and field gig requests and phone calls and emails, to say, "yes," "no," "what's this about, where, when?" . . . I believe the case to be when people can have direct access to you, it sort of diminishes your bargaining power. . . . I may be 100 percent wrong, but the way I see it and conduct business, you're sort of lessened a bit when people can talk with you, you're kind of vulnerable. If they can argue with you about price, it's not a good look.

The artist should not do that back-and-forth, they should see you when you get onstage. It's not about the artist being a diva. . . . You set up a position and should position yourself in a way where you don't have people getting to you. I have an artist rep now, not a manager, per se. I know how much I want to make, I know how to read a contract, get flights booked, etc. I have my reps deal with the promoters. It's *impossible* to find representation and impossible to find one where that's all they do. Most start off having day gigs before some are able to transition to management full-time. There are a few good booking agents in jazz and too many managers. It's important to have a team that works with you. As artists, it's important to do the music. We need to concentrate on the music, deal with the musicians, show up onstage, and give a great performance. If you have to negotiate with money, no, musicians shouldn't have to deal with that; to me, it's kind of demeaning. . . . Tell it to my rep who fields the details to give me; they don't have to tell me about the back-and-forth. It can get pretty ugly.

For the most part, classical musicians do not require management. Dorothy Lawson did not need a manager personally:

I have, as an individual, never had a manager. . . . When we began, we reached out to a young company that specialized in representing composers, when we were only one year old. It was a nontraditional arrangement, but they saw the relevance. . . . ETHEL is an organization that sustains itself through great writing, management and outreach, educational opportunities. We have a board of directors and financial advisor. ICM just signed us and sent us out to bigger venues. Management provides access to a level of presenters you can't get to without them. Presenters need a short form to navigate. As an individual, I have lived by the phone.

HOW TO FIND A MANAGER

This can be a little tricky. Jeff Clayton told me, "In jazz, a person can get out of jail, print up business cards, and call himself a manager; no credentials are required." James Browne, who managed artists, was equally cynical: "In pop, there is only *one* level, and that is the top. You are either Britney Spears, or you work in Barnes & Noble. In rock and roll, there are managers with whom I was highly suspect of their ability to *read*! Artists should look at what the person has done; they must have a track record." Do your homework. Talk to artists who left the agency and find out why they left. Tia Fuller is one of several artists who was ripped off for a substantial amount of money by a manager (eventually, her manager paid her back). Reach out to industry folks and find out about their interactions with managers.

It took Ulysses Owens several years before he connected with Myles Weinstein, first as a booking agent, now as his manager. He'd met Myles years ago when he was booking Russell Malone (Ulysses was in Russell's band). A year or so after that meeting, Ulysses expressed interest in working with him, but Myles recognized that he wasn't ready at that time. Over the years, he'd see Ulysses play with others, but it was his *Songs of Freedom* project that got Myles's attention. He recounts, "Myles represents Alicia Olatuja, who is part of the project. He came to the premiere at the Appel Room and expressed his excitement, said he really loved the project; called a few days later to ask if I believed in it enough to tour with it. He saw that the project has legs . . . it went from there." The manager/artist relationship requires trust, enthusiasm, and honesty. With Myles, Ulysses has all three.

THE AGENT

Tia Fuller, who has had three managers including Margo Davis, her friend from Spelman ("Everyone needs a Margo in their lives, she's a diehard friend and will do whatever it takes to elevate you as a friend."), acknowledges that "Everyone needs a booking agent." She hires such people as needed. She goes on to explain that you need "somebody who will give you work and the visibility for managers or publicists to do whatever, but if you're not out there with the product, and doing what you do for that project, it's hard to promote [you]. . . . I had been looking for agents, no one was pulling. It wasn't until 2009 when I landed the *JazzTimes* cover, then people wanted to sign me. They wanted to jump on a train that's already in motion."

Each genre has its own demands. Aaron Diehl works in both jazz and classical. For classical, he is a client of Opus 3, which he says is "doing a great job creating relationships[, having] me appear in these orchestras about six to eight times/year, which is nice." Regarding agents, however, he is somewhat critical of the differences between the jazz side versus classical. He suggests that "there's a stark difference" between the jazz and classical business models:

> [Because of] the institutional money that classical music has, the people generally are better at their jobs—they get paid properly. Opus 3 has a team of people who work at the company. They have offices in New York, Los Angeles, and Berlin. I have a manager at the agency who has an assistant and someone who advances the tour, etc. With the fees they get as a company, they're able to hire people who are competent at what they do. Jazz: hard to find an agent, the fees people are getting are not good, in comparison. . . . I'm happy with my manager, Andre Guess, Ed Arrendell does good stuff, but there are few out there. If you went to Harvard, for example, and have a skill set, why go into jazz and starve? The supply and demand of the industry: you have a few who can make a decent living. You have artists like Chick Corea, Herbie Hancock, or Robert Glasper, but those people are a handful, and the funding isn't there for jazz. If you're a young artist and getting so many gigs and have so much potential, you need someone to manage your business and bookings, but don't just get anybody. It's how you position yourself.

NOTES

- Know the difference between a manager and a booking agent.
- Consider getting a personal assistant before you search for a manager.
- Managers are not easy to find.
- You have to have something *to* manage.
- Bring together a team as needed.

PART SIX
THE EMPTY-VESSEL THEORY

We study the past to understand the present;
we understand the present to guide the future.
—William Lund

CHAPTER 19

Ancestors: So Past, So Present—Standing on Their Shoulders

Know whence you came. If you know whence you came,
there is really no limit on where you can go.
—James Baldwin

I will always remember June 16, 1997. That was the day when Randy Weston walked into MNN studios for our scheduled interview. He and I had met briefly the week before when I stepped in front of him at a jazz function as he exited the stage. Struck by his 6-foot, 7-inch frame and majestic smile, I was not prepared for what was to follow. For one hour, he talked about Mother Africa and the ancestors. He shared stories of his early encounters with Thelonious Monk and Max Roach and beamed with pride when he talked of his father and mother. Twenty years later, I had the good fortune to interview him, again at WBGO. With little sign of age, at ninety-one he was as exuberant as ever. On September 1, 2018, Randy joined the ancestors whom he loved and revered to his own death. In life, Randy passed on the knowledge given to him, and he, in turn, blessed us with his wisdom. For those of us who were fortunate to have walked this Earth with Randy, we are forever grateful. Likewise, I am honored to have known the musicians, interviewed in the first edition, who have passed, and this is why I am including excerpts from them in the second edition. It is on their shoulders that we stand. They learned from their elders; now they are ours. Music is created in a coveted place, for those who are open and aware enough to accept the creation. Oscar Brown Jr., Ruth Brown, Edwin Hawkins, Al Jarreau, John Levy, David Randolph, and Dr. Billy Taylor, like links on a chain, as beacons of light, they connect us with our past and guide us to the future.

I never had the opportunity to meet Monk, Miles, Trane, or Duke, but I cherish the stories from those who did. Michael Wolff worked with so many great musicians, such as Sonny Rollins, Cannonball Adderley, and Cal Tjader, and knew the importance of passing down information:

> Miles Davis is the good virus, as opposed to the bad virus. All of the people who played with him got good. He got it from whoever he played with—Dizzy, Bird. It was magic, passing down a tradition and point of view of constantly being creative and changing. Although I met Miles, I never played with him, but I played with Sonny, Cannonball. All the people who played with him, they passed it down. You can listen to records and play the music, but you got to meet them. I'm about the soul and what's underneath the music. I worked with a lot of different people, but I ask specific things like from Bill Evans. Then he let me watch him practice, sit behind him; it was sort of the harmonic approach, his touch that I loved.

Lessons come from many directions. Olu Dara said, "You don't watch [others] to copy; you watch to see what not to do. People have to use life as a gauge of what not to do." Oscar Brown Jr. got advice that he did not follow: "I went to Ahmad Jamal and asked him how to get into show biz, and he said, go back to real estate. He told me that before he did *Live at the Pershing*. Max Roach talked about owning your own publishing." Ruth Brown, too, had the benefit of her elders:

"I knew them all. They'd tell me, as a compliment, but it was *good stuff*. Billie Holiday said, 'Find your own way'; Nat King Cole, 'Make sure people understand every line you are saying, every line you are singing. Speak clearly.' And, Lena Horne: 'Be classy. Look your best because people came to see you.'"

OSCAR BROWN JR.

Oscar Brown Jr. knew the vicissitudes of fame. His production *Kicks and Company* was much anticipated and supported.

> Mr. Kicks was a character who worked for the devil. I started on the song, then I decided it would make a good play. Later I saw some kids in jail in the South who had participated in the sit-in movement. Then I got the idea for him [Mr. Kicks] to corrupt them, and it took me a couple of years to write it because I had to develop the story. I was new at it. The characters started to take over, and I had a big fight with them about where they wanted to go. Plus, I was writing songs, and I had to make them up to fit the story. The agents came around, and Joe Glaser, who had managed Louis Armstrong, booked me on the *Today Show*, and I was quite a sensation. Dave Garroway was so impressed he came to see me at the Village Vanguard, and the set he saw was me performing six to eight of the songs from *Kicks*, and he offered me two hours on the *Today Show*, the *whole* show. Woody King said they passed a *Kicks and Company* law so that would not happen again. I don't know if that is true, though. It was way ahead of its time . . . so it did not run long. My ego got deflated *so* fast by the time *Kicks and Company* was over. It was nine months from beginning to end (January to October), and I had to have a comeback. People walked away from me; it was a stinker, and they did not put it on their résumé. I did the best I could, just a whole lot of illusions, and you

don't know that if you've never been there. It is not like Cinderella.

Does not mean you can't have new illusions. I was thirty-four, I was a big boy, I had been kicked out of college, the Communist party—I was too black to be red— the U.S. Army, so I *knew* how to take rejection. I'd been kicked off the air frequently when I was a broadcaster, so that was no sweat. As I said before, I was always too conceited to commit suicide, so when you get that out of the way, things take care of themselves.

On success and failure regarding *Kicks and Company*: Oscar Brown Jr. got that early in his career when he wrote the play *Kicks and Company*. It was a major production, but in essence, it flopped and never made it to Broadway. The story goes:

> Opening night was in Chicago and was a benefit for the Urban League; we packed the five-thousand-seat house. Black people loved it, yet, we never got to New York City. When we opened, the critics called it "amateur night in Dixie," and "pelvic choreography." The dancing was based on the Twist—we wanted to use the dance that the kids were doing. But it was the dance that the black kids were doing. A couple weeks later, the dance hit in the cities.

"How did you feel?" I asked (maybe a dumb question, since he'd already told me it was a painful subject).

He laughed his big, hearty laugh and said,

> In my act I used to tell the audience: "I wrote a play that was supposed to be a big hit, but instead, it closed in four days." Then I'd sing a little of the music from the play. Then I'd tell the audience, "People came up to me after that flop and asked me, 'How do you feel?'" Those are the kind of people who stop at traffic accidents and say, "Ooh,

look at that!" Then I'd say, "Yeah, but I was cool," and perform my song "But I Was Cool." I spent two years working
on that thing; it was heartbreaking, but it was very educational. I found that failure in something is what you have
to accept. Success can be thrust upon you and frequently
is. A lot of people don't deserve it but get it anyway. Failure
was a damn good lesson to me. The whole thing was so,
by the time I walked through there, I had had an education in theater, and it cost $400,000, which was a lot more
money than is spent on the education of most nations. I
had to pay back the 3,300 bucks of the money advanced to
me. It was quite a thing to be in *Time* Magazine and *Life*
Magazine; it was big-time. This was all in eight months
from beginning to end.

RUTH BROWN

On Survival

I asked Ruth how she had been able to survive the industry and how
she was able to stay motivated. Her answer:

My love of my children. It was my choice to stop work.
I came off the road and my baby, Earl, was in my mother's arms, and he screamed when I went to hold him. So I
said, "*That's it*; I'm not going anywhere else." Only place
for me to work was Mount Vernon, or in the Baby Grand
[Harlem], local stuff. You got to be out there, or, out of
sight, out of mind. I was out from about 1965 to 1976. I
had no problems doing a nine-to-five job. I worked all my
life. I'm the oldest of seven children; I've been working all
of my life. When I worked in Long Island, I used my married name, Blount. I worked for Head Start, I was driving a
bus, cleaning homes; I was Ruth Blount. During one Black
History Month, I was cleaning a house, and the radio was
on, and I heard the disc jockey talking about rhythm and

blues. He said, "When they write the history of R&B, this lady's name will be right up at the top." He started playing my music. So I said, "*Where's my money?!*" That is when I started this fight to get my royalties.

On Spearheading Fight for Royalties

Ruth Brown was not one of the lucky ones to get a good contract. In her book, *Miss Rhythm: The Autobiography of Ruth Brown, Rhythm & Blues Legend,* you can read in detail the story of her twenty-two-year fight with Atlantic Records to get her royalties. She led the struggle, not just for herself, but for other artists who had been denied their money. Ruth signed with Atlantic in 1949 while she was in the hospital recovering from a car accident. At that point, the company had been in hard times but was moving up a bit. Without the advice of anyone except her manager, Ruth signed a contract that gave her an advance of $69 (years later, it was increased to $350) a side, and she was responsible for certain production costs. With all of her gold records, she could not understand why she had no money from her music.

She said, "It took me twenty-two years to get royalties. My lawyer, Howell Begle, did the work, not me. After an engagement, he brought my albums for me to sign, and I asked him where he got them. He said that he had paid dearly for them, and I told him I wasn't getting a penny for those records. I had not gotten a penny for my records in over thirty years. I told him I was not the only one who had not gotten any money." Although Ruth and the other musicians who fought for the royalties never got all of what they were owed, the music industry came up with some money. In Ruth's case, some of her settlement was used as the seed money to set up the Rhythm and Blues Foundation.

Showtime had my book for almost two years. My story was supposed to be made into a movie, but at the last minute, for some reason, someone stopped it. I believe that it was Atlantic; *I named names!* The truth was there. They still owe me money, but they claim that they can't find the papers. They say that they sent the papers to Virginia, but I have not lived there in over fifty-five years, and the house is no longer there. When it was over, I got about 20K, but when I got it, I owed everybody. No one ever taught me how to invest my money. A lot of us did the same things; we had husbands who ended up being our managers, but that did not work. Now my son Earl Swanson manages me.

It took almost the entire music community to get Atlantic to pay Ruth and other musicians monies they were due. Politicians who happened to be music fans—if not her fans—and other visible artists, like Bonnie Raitt, rallied behind Ruth.

EDWIN HAWKINS

Edwin Hawkins understands the pressures of success very well. In his twenties, his rendition of "Oh Happy Day" became what was considered an overnight sensation, taking gospel music to the secular world. When I asked him how he handled the pressures of success, he responded,

There are pressures. I remember very well. Like Buddha Records trying to take another song and make it into something with the magnitude of "Oh Happy Day." You cannot re-create that. I believe that God did it alone. We recorded it on a two-track machine in a church; what was the likelihood of that happening again? People understood the component of a successful record, but to recreate that is a greater challenge.

The church world, especially the black church here in the Bay Area, was upset that it was played on secular radio. I heard that there was a group of ministers who had petitioned to get it off the secular radio. That was very confusing to me. They had always taught us to take the gospel into the world, and this was being done. The reaction was very strange. When it became a hit, the gospel DJs tried to take credit for it becoming a hit, though the secular DJs played it first.

AL JARREAU

Al Jarreau talked extensively about his songwriting—putting words to Chick Corea's "Spain" and Joe Zawinul's "A Remark You Made."

Melody comes first. My advice to people who work with words, even many who say they have written a lyric, it may be that they have written poetry, but not necessarily a lyric. I think that 99 percent of songwriting happens with melody first, some sort of musical stuff is going on first. It is an interesting process when it begins somewhere else. Take the 23rd Psalm, for example. It existed long before music was put to it. You got an unorthodox piece of music, which makes it novel, unusual, and may be very attractive in that regard. [Jarreau sings the psalm, which gives me goose bumps.] That is unusual writing and *powerful* because that person had to work with a poem that was already written. Because that person was so sincere, he figured out how to make the climax of the song. He wrote that in so it would be at the end of the prayer, which is the climax of the song and makes everything that leads up to that moment. The poem has been there a long, long time.

I just finished a lyric for the Bach "Air on a G String"; it's a pretty good lyric, what *balls* I got to go straight for Bach. It took balls for someone to go and write this lyric to Chick Corea or Joe Zawinul and Weather Report, "A Remark You Made." I wrote lyrics for it because it was a brilliant piece of music and I wanted to perform it, and I did not want to stand in front of the audience like a horn player and just sing a melody. It took about eight months to write the lyrics. I wanted it to be relevant, and I wanted to have something to say.

Keep Striving

Five-time Grammy Award–winner Al Jarreau says,

> You are never *there*. It is how you think about it. You can never think that you have arrived. That is the adult, healthy way to think about it. Whether you are talking about your growth as an athlete or growth as a Buddhist monk, you should always be reaching, striving for another level. If you don't love it enough to do it for free, you might want to think of doing something else. If you love it like that, you'll find a way. I have not had a huge rip-roaring success. I'll accept the limited number of people who want to hear me do it the way I want to do it. I think that there is something valuable about what I do, and I can't help it. I'm going to do it in this particular way. At some point, I might be left with having to do it at the Holiday Inn. I started there, and I'll go back there. I didn't make much money then. The love gives you the longevity, and it gives you the courage to do it during hard times. If you love it, you constantly are finding new things in it—the new you that you are excited about being today. If you think that you've made it, you won't keep looking for the new you that will keep you excited about the craft.

JOHN LEVY

John Levy had the benefit of age (he was ninety-seven at the time of our interview) to see what has and has not changed in the business.

> When I came along, you almost had to book in order to get your artist to a certain stage in the business; then you turned them over to a booking agency, who at that

time represented a certain class of entertainers/musicians. There were booking agencies that worked with people and helped develop their careers. That's all gone today. Now it's all about promotion. Artists need lawyers or people who promote an artist to get them in the marketplace on a certain level; these people don't necessarily have any experience about where they should play or what they should do. There is an entity for each one of these things; not one person can do it all. Even me, I was capable of booking, managing. I knew all of the places and where to play; I knew the promoters, the entrepreneurs personally, because I had been out there. You can't operate that way anymore today; you need a lawyer, a manager who you can trust and know the business, a booking agent. If you don't have all three, you are floundering on our own. Anybody who is anybody has all three.

DAVID RANDOLPH

David Randolph found out the hard way that personal contact is important. While trying to gain some funds for the St. Cecelia Chorus, he looked through the grant book of the Foundation Center for foundations that would be suitable to give money to what St. Cecelia Chorus was doing. In going over the grant qualifications, he noticed the words "personal contact desirable." So he wrote letters to seventy-five foundations. "Sixty did not answer or said no. We knew no one. After ten to twelve years of inviting a man in charge of a foundation—he came to every concert—we got a $2,000 grant. That is the way it happens when you don't know anyone."

DR. BILLY TAYLOR

Here are some snippets from an interview I conducted with Dr. Billy Taylor.

Sheila E. Anderson: What are you sure you don't know?

Dr. Billy Taylor: I'm sure I don't know enough to make things the way I'd like for them to be. I thought I was smart and had a handle on things in the cultural sense and the musical sense. I thought that if I did my job, everything would turn out OK. It does not work that way. There are some possibilities in life; as it changes, you can't have that kind of control. The closest you can do is take the things around you and try to influence them for the better.

Sheila E. Anderson: I observed that musicians under forty, for the most part, don't see themselves as entertainers.

Dr. Billy Taylor: That is a mistake. I try to tell everybody who comes on with me, people who ask my advice, I tell them, "You are in show business." There are things you must do about your appearance, your demeanor; it's not just about sitting at the piano or singing.

Dr. Billy Taylor (remembering an experience early in his career): Musicians still have to fight for money. Sure, we all did. I had a trio on the road. I had put the gig in Rochester; I was proud of myself. I had put two gigs together; I was going to play there, then go to Chicago. The guy did not pay me in Rochester, New York. So, I called my father for money because I could not get to Chicago otherwise. He sent me the money. We had a contract. I went to the union, and the guy copped out on me and said he could not do anything for me. They were supposed to protect me. It's still the same today.

The end, for now!

About the Author

Sheila E. Anderson is an on-air personality on WBGO, Newark, 88.3 FM—the most popular jazz station in the country—and hosts *Weekend Jazz After Hours, Salon Sessions*, and the *Sunday Night Music Mix*. She currently curates the Jazz in the Garden series for the Newark Museum and the Central Jersey Jazz Festival. Anderson graduated from Baruch College with a bachelor of arts degree in English. She lectures on jazz history and is a 2014 Columbia University Community Scholar. She lives in New York City.

Index

Books from Allworth Press

Acting the Song (Second Edition)
by Tracey Moore with Allison Bergman (6 × 9, 336 pages, paperback, $24.99)

Guitar Amplifier Encyclopedia
by Brian Tarquin (8½ × 11, 140 pages, paperback, $19.99)

Guitar Encyclopedia
by Brian Tarquin (8½ × 11, 256 pages, paperback, $29.95)

How Music Dies (or Lives)
by Ian Brennan (6 × 9, 426 pages, paperback, $19.99)

The Insider's Guide to Home Recording
by Brian Tarquin (5½ × 8¼, 224 pages, paperback, $16.95)

The Insider's Guide to Music Licensing
by Brian Tarquin (6 × 9, 256 pages, paperback, $19.95)

Leadership in the Performing Arts
by Tobie S. Stein (5½ × 8¼, 252 pages, paperback, $19.99)

Legal Guide to Social Media
by Kimberly A. Houser (6 × 9, 208 pages, paperback, $19.95)

Managing Artists in Pop Music (Second Edition)
by Mitch Weiss and Perri Gaffney (6 × 9, 288 pages, paperback, $19.95)

Performing Arts Management
by Tobie S. Stein and Jessica Bathurst (8½ × 11, 552 pages, paperback, $50.00)

The Quotable Musician
by Sheila E. Anderson (7½ × 7½ , 224 pages, paperback, $16.95)

Singing in Musical Theatre
by Joan Melton (6 × 9, 240 pages, paperback, $19.95)

Starting Your Career as a Musician
by Neil Tortorella (6 × 9, 240 pages, paperback, $19.95)

Starting Your Career in Voice-Overs
by Talon Beeson (6 × 9, 208 pages, paperback, $16.95)

Succeed with Social Media Like a Creative Genius™
by Brainard Carey (6⅛ × 6⅛, 144 pages, paperback, $12.99)

There's Money Where Your Mouth Is (Fourth Edition)
by Elaine A. Clark (6 × 9, 360 pages, paperback, $24.99)

VO (Second Edition)
by Harlan Hogan (6 × 9, 256 pages, paperback, $19.95)

Voiceovers (Second Edition)
by Janet Wilcox (6 × 9, 208 pages, paperback, $19.95)

Your Child's Career in Music and Entertainment
by Steven C. Beer with Kathryne Badura (5½ × 8¼, 184 pages, paperback, $14.99)

To see our complete catalog or to order online, please visit *www.allworth.com*.